SCHOLASTIC

Follow-the-Directions
Math Story Mats

by Ada Goren

New York • Toronto • London • Auckland • Sydney
Mexico City • New Delhi • Hong Kong • Buenos Aires

Teaching *Resources*

Produced and edited by Immacula A. Rhodes
Cover design by Maria Lilja
Interior design by Sydney Wright
Illustrations by Teresa Anderko, Maxie Chambliss, Rusty Fletcher,
James Graham Hale, Anne Kennedy, and Sydney Wright

ISBN: 978-0-545-28072-3

2 3 4 5 6 7 8 9 10   40   18 17 16 15 14 13 12

Contents

About This Book

Making sure children grasp essential math skills is so important! Research shows that understanding math concepts is fundamental to developing proficiency and becoming an autonomous learner. The activities in *Follow-the-Directions: Math Story Mats* provide a refreshing way to help children explore and build understanding of critical math concepts, such as shapes, patterns, addition, subtraction, fractions, measurement, and more.

The interactive, reproducible math story activities in this book are designed to meet the needs of your class. Children simply listen to a math-related, read-aloud story and use manipulatives to follow along and solve the problems presented. In addition to promoting math exploration, listening skills, and following directions, the stories help children deepen their thinking about math concepts and become confident learners. Accompanying the math story mats are discussion questions and easy-to-play games that reinforce and extend learning, as well as tips to help you assess children's math skills. Activities are linked to one or more of the National Council of Teachers of Mathematics (NCTM) standards and the Math Common Core State Standards. (See Meeting the Math Standards, page 6.)

Everything you need for the story-mat activities and corresponding games is here and ready to assemble. You can use the activities for instruction with the whole class, small groups, student pairs, or individuals. They're also great for learning centers. Whether you want children to practice addition or subtraction skills, create patterns, or learn about time and money concepts, you'll find a story mat activity in this resource that fits the need and makes math meaningful and fun!

What's Inside

To enhance learning and build important math skills, the following features are included in each lesson:

* an introductory page for the teacher that provides a materials list and directions on how to prepare and use the read-aloud story-mat activity and story-mat game

* discussion questions that reinforce and extend learning

* suggestions on ways to assess children's learning

* a reproducible, read-aloud story and step-by-step game directions

* a reproducible story mat

* reproducible manipulatives needed for the read-aloud story-mat activity and story-mat game—such as picture or number cards, game cube or spinner, or rulers

Introducing the Story-Mat Activities

The read-aloud story activities may be presented to the whole class, small groups, student pairs, or individual children. The story-mat games are designed for small groups of two to four children. Before presenting the read-aloud story or story-mat game, decide on the size of the group you'll be working with and prepare enough materials for each child in the group. (Check the materials list for the desired activity. Note that for some activities, you may need easy-to-find supplies, such as a die, brass fastener, paper clip, or crayons.) Keep in mind that, in most cases, you can prepare and use the same story mats for both the story and game activities.

When introducing the read-aloud story activity, begin by reading the story as children listen quietly. Then read the story again, inviting children to place and move the manipulatives on and off their mats to solve the problems presented in the story. When finished, encourage them to discuss the story and share their problem-solving strategies. Use the questions in Talk About It as a follow-up to help children demonstrate and verbalize their understanding of the math concepts. If desired, you might come up with additional problems to go with the story.

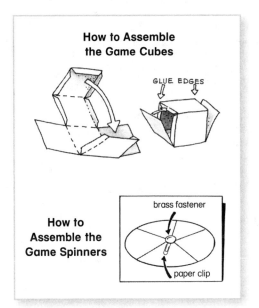

The companion story-mat game offers additional practice in the targeted skill. Demonstrate how to set up and play the game before having children play it independently. The games are ideal for center activities.

 Helpful Tips

✳ To make the story mats and game spinners sturdier, you might copy the patterns onto tagboard.

✳ Store the read-aloud story and story-mat game components in a large resealable plastic bag. Label the bag with the name of the activity.

✳ Place each individual set of cards in separate resealable sandwich bags to keep the cards sorted.

✳ Before playing the game, help children determine the order in which players take turns, such as rolling a die and going in numerical order, or taking turns in the order of their birthdays.

✳ Feel free to customize or adapt the stories and games to meet the needs of your class. For example, you can provide children with 18 bone cards for Lucky Dog! and then present problems that involve addition to 18.

✳ Create your own math-related stories and problems for children to solve with their mats and manipulatives. You might also invite children to make up stories or simple problems for classmates to solve.

Connections to the NCTM Math Standards

The activities in this book are designed to support you in meeting the following K–2 standards—including process standards, such as problem solving, reasoning and proof, and communication—recommended by the National Council of Teachers of Mathematics (NCTM):

Numbers and Operations

Understand numbers, ways of representing numbers, relationships among numbers, and number systems

• Count with understanding and recognize "how many" in sets of objects

• Develop understanding of the relative position and magnitude of whole numbers and of ordinal and cardinal numbers and their connections

Understand meanings of operations and how they relate to one another

• Understand various meanings of addition and subtraction of whole numbers

• Understand the effects of adding and subtracting whole numbers

Compute fluently and make reasonable estimates

• Develop and use strategies for whole-number computation, with a focus on addition and subtraction

• Develop fluency with basic number combinations for addition and subtraction

• Use a variety of methods and tools to compute, including objects, mental computation, and paper and pencil

Algebra

Understands patterns, relations, and functions

• Recognize, describe, and extend patterns

• Analyze how repeating patterns are generated

Use mathematical models to represent and understand quantitative relationships

• Model situations that involve the addition and subtraction of whole numbers, using objects, pictures, and symbols

Geometry

Analyze characteristics and properties of two- and three-dimensional geometric shapes

• Recognize, name, compare, and sort two- and three-dimensional shapes

• Describe attributes and parts of two- and three-dimensional shapes

Measurement

Understand measurable attributes of objects and the units, systems, and processes of measurement

• Recognize the attributes of length and time

• Understand how to measure using nonstandard and standard units

Apply appropriate techniques, tools, and formulas to determine measurement

• Measure with multiple copies of units of the same size, such as paper clips

• Use tools to measure

Data Analysis and Probability

Formulate questions that can be addressed with data and collect, organize, and display relevant data to answer them

• Sort and classify objects according to their attributes and organize data about the objects

• Represent data using concrete objects, pictures, and graphs

Source: National Council of Teachers of Mathematics. (2000). *Principles and Standards for School Mathematics.* Reston, VA: NCTM. www.nctm.org.

Meeting the Common Core Standards for Mathematics

The activities in this book will also help you meet your specific state mathematics standards as well as those recommended by the CCSSI. These materials address the following common core standards for students in grades K–2. For more information, go to the website of the CCSSI: www.corestandards.org.

Counting & Cardinality

• K.CC.1. Count to 100 by ones and by tens.

• K.CC.4. Understand the relationship between numbers and quantities.

• K.CC.6. Identify whether the number of objects in one group is greater than, less than, or equal to the number of objects in another group.

Operations & Algebraic Thinking

• K.OA.1, 1.OA.1, 2.OA.1: Use addition and subtraction within 20 to solve word problems involving situations of adding to, taking from, putting together, taking apart, and comparing, with unknowns in all positions.

Number & Operations in Base Ten

• K.NBT.1. Compose and decompose numbers from 11 to 19 into ten ones and some further ones; understand that these numbers are composed of ten ones and one, two, three, four, five, six, seven, eight, or nine ones.

• 1.NBT.2. Understand that the two digits of a two-digit number represent amounts of tens and ones.

• 2.NBT.1. Understand that the three digits of a three-digit number represent amounts of hundreds, tens, and ones.

Measurement & Data

• K.MD.3. Classify objects into given categories; count the numbers of objects in each category and sort the categories by count.

• 1.MD.2. Express the length of an object as a whole number of length units, by laying multiple copies of a shorter object (the length unit) end to end; understand that the length measurement of an object is the number of same-size length units that span it with no gaps or overlaps.

• 1.MD.3. Tell and write time in hours and half-hours using analog and digital clocks.

• 1.MD.4. Organize, represent, and interpret data with up to three categories; ask and answer questions about the total number of data points, how many in each category, and how many more or less are in one category than in another.

• 2.MD.4. Measure to determine how much longer one object is than another, expressing the length difference in terms of a standard length unit.

• 2.MD.8. Solve word problems involving dollar bills, quarters, dimes, nickels, and pennies, using $ and ¢ symbols appropriately.

Geometry

• K.G.2. Correctly name shapes regardless of their orientations or overall size.

• 1.G.1, 2.G.1: Recognize and draw shapes having specified attributes, such as a given number of angles or a given number of equal faces.

• 2.G.3. Partition circles and rectangles into two, three, or four equal shares, describe the shares using the words halves, thirds, half of, a third of, etc., and describe the whole as two halves, three thirds, four fourths.

Bev's Bake Shop

Read-Aloud Story

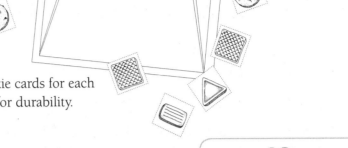

Materials

read-aloud story (page 8)
story mat (page 9)
cookie cards (page 10)

Getting Ready

Copy, color, and cut out a story mat and a set of cookie cards for each child in a small group. Laminate the mats and cards for durability.

Using the Story Mat

Give each child a story mat and a set of cookie cards. Ask children to listen as you read aloud the story the first time. Then read the story again. Pause as you go along, giving children time to use their mats and cards to solve the problems.

Talk About It

✳ How did you decide which cookies to use for the last order?

✳ Can you think of a cookie shape with more than four sides?

Story-Mat Game

Materials (for 2–4 players)

game directions (page 8)
story mat (page 9)
cookie cards (page 10)

Getting Ready

Copy, cut out, and laminate the game directions. Use the story mats and cookie cards that were prepared for the story-mat activity, or prepare additional cards for the game.

Playing the Game

Give each player a story mat. Shuffle the cookie cards and pass out six cards facedown to each player. Tell players that they should not look at their cards at this time. Stack the remaining cards facedown in the middle of the table. Then read the game directions and model how to play the game. If desired, play it with children the first time.

Assessment TIPS

• Check for children's ability to identify the cookie shapes by name.

• Observe to see if children identify the cookie shapes by their attributes.

• During the game, check that children correctly match the cookie shapes.

Bev's Bake Shop

Welcome to Bev's Bake Shop! Today Bev has several cookie orders she needs to box up for her customers. For the first order, she needs 4 square cookies and 4 circle cookies. Help Bev make a row of cookies for each shape. Great!

Now clear the cookies off of the mat. It's time for Bev to make up the second order. She needs 2 square cookies, 2 triangle cookies, and 2 circle cookies. Put the cookies in the box. Which cookie shape has the most sides?

Clear the mat for the third order. Bev needs 3 rectangle cookies, 2 square cookies, and 3 circle cookies. Put the cookies in the box. How many of the cookies have four sides? Are all of those cookies the same shape?

It's time to clear the mat for the last order. Bev needs an equal number of cookies with three sides and cookies with four sides. What cookie shapes will you put in the box? How many of each shape did you put in this order?

Bev's Bake Shop

Players: 2–4

How to Play

1. Turn over your cards. Do you have any matching pairs? If so, name the shape of the cookies in that pair. Then set the pair aside.

2. Take a card from the stack. What shape is the cookie?

3. Does it match any of your remaining cookies?
   • If so, place the matching pair aside.
   • If not, put the card at the bottom of the stack.

4. Keep taking turns. Players remove each matching pair that they make during their turn. The first player to use all of his or her cards wins the game.

Follow-the-Directions Math Story Mats © 2012 by Ada Goren, Scholastic Teaching Resources

Bev's Bake Shop

Cookie Cards

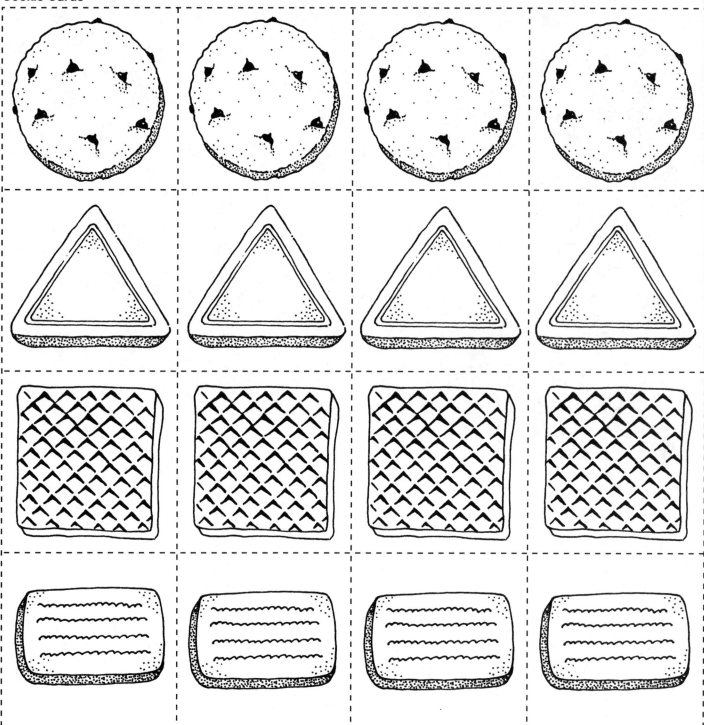

Mrs. Landry's Laundry

Read-Aloud Story

Materials

read-aloud story (page 12)
story mat (page 13)
clothes cards (page 14)

Getting Ready

Copy, color, and cut out the story mat and two sets of clothing cards for each child in a small group. Laminate the mats and cards for durability.

Using the Story Mat

Give each child a story mat and two sets of clothing cards. Ask children to listen as you read aloud the story the first time. Then read the story again. Pause as you go along, giving children time to use their mats and cards to solve the problems.

Talk About It

❋ How did you decide which clothes were needed to continue each pattern?

❋ Which pattern was the easiest to continue? Why?

❋ Which was the most difficult pattern to continue? Why?

Assessment TIPS

• Check that children read the patterns from left to right.

• Determine whether children can match their clothing cards to the items on the clothesline.

• Observe if children correctly extend the patterns as they complete the story-mat activity or play the game.

Story-Mat Game

Materials (for 2–4 players)

game directions (page 12)
story mat (page 13)
clothing cards (page 14)
pattern strips (pages 14–15)

Getting Ready

Copy and cut out the game directions and one set of the pattern strips. Color the pattern strips (if desired), then laminate all of the pieces. Use the story mats and clothing cards that were prepared for the story-mat activity, or prepare additional cards for the game.

Playing the Game

Give each player a story mat and a pattern strip. Shuffle and stack the clothing cards facedown in the middle of the table. Then read the directions and model how to play the game. If desired, play it with children the first time.

Mrs. Landry's Laundry

Mrs. Landry had lots of laundry this week! Each day, she hung her laundry on the clothesline to make a pattern.

On Monday, she hung up a pair of pants, then a shirt, pants, and shirt. What did she hang up next? Place cards on the line to continue the pattern.

On Tuesday, Mrs. Landry hung up a skirt, then a sock, skirt, and sock. Hang clothes on the line to continue the pattern.

On Wednesday, she made a different kind of pattern. She hung up a shirt, then 2 socks. What do you think came next? Hang it on the line. Then continue the pattern.

On Thursday, Mrs. Landry hung up a pair of pants, a skirt, and a shirt. Then she hung up another pair of pants. Hang up the two things that come next in her pattern.

On Friday, Mrs. Landry had 3 shirts, 3 pants, and 4 socks in her laundry basket. Hang 6 of the clothes on the line to make your own pattern.

Mrs. Landry's Laundry

Players: 2–4

How to Play

1. Take the top card from the stack. What item is on the card?

2. Can you use it to continue the pattern on your pattern strip?
   - If so, "hang" it on your clothesline.
   - If not, put the card at the bottom of the stack.

3. Players keep taking turns, hanging clothes on their clothesline from left to right to continue their pattern. The first player to hang six cards wins the game.

Follow-the-Directions Math Story Mats © 2012 by Ada Goren, Scholastic Teaching Resources

Mrs. Landry's Laundry Story Mat

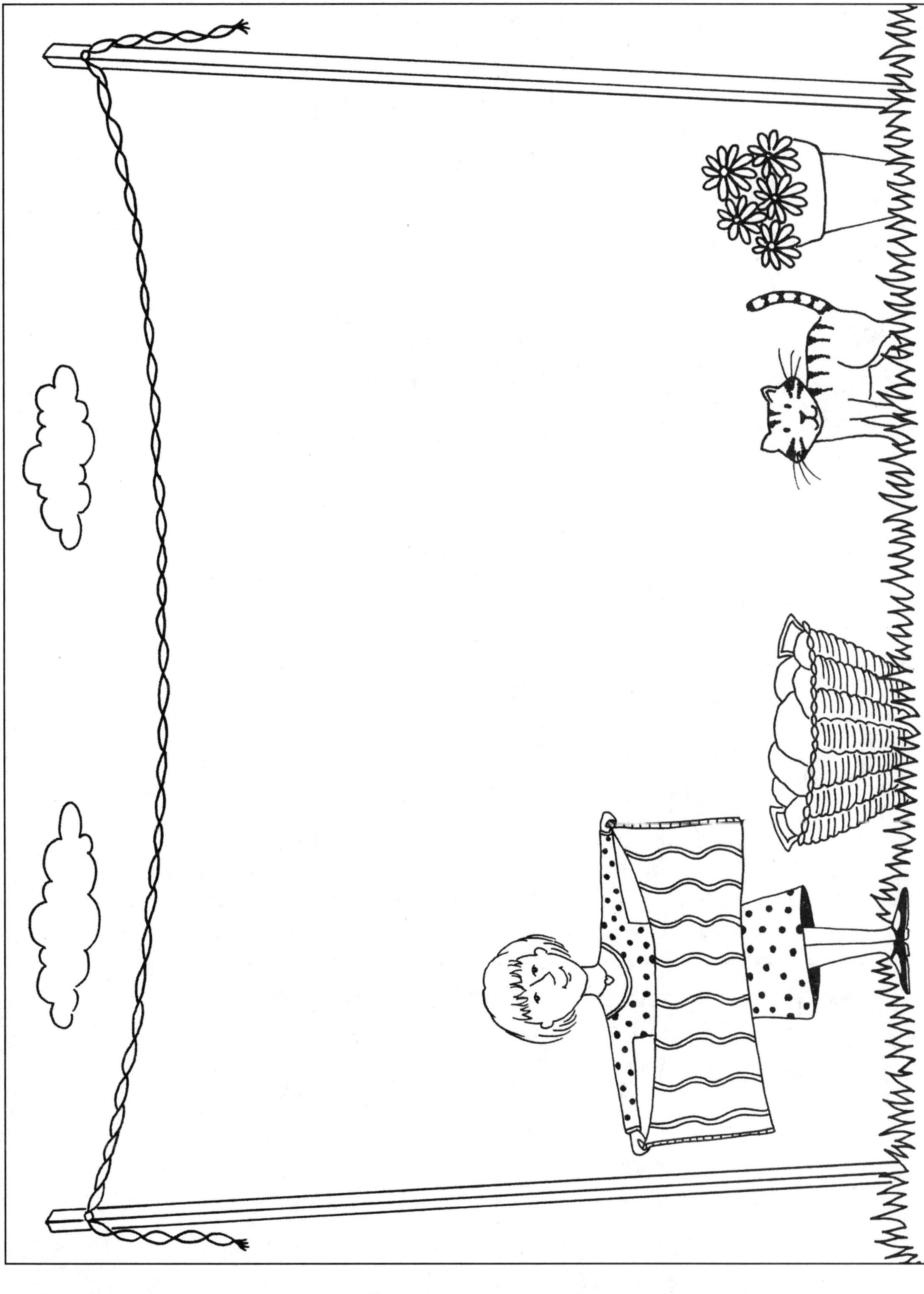

Clothing Cards and Pattern Strips

Pattern Strips

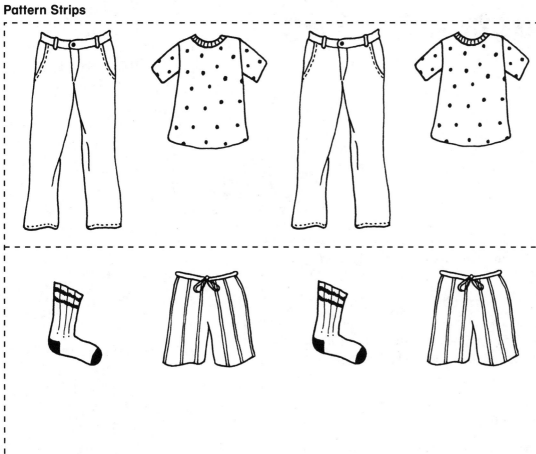

The Button Basket

Materials

read-aloud story (page 17)
story mat (page 18)
button cards (page 19)

Getting Ready

Copy, color, and cut out a copy of the story mat and a set of button cards for each child in a small group. Laminate the mats and cards for durability.

Using the Story Mat

Give each child a story mat and a set of button cards. Ask children to listen as you read aloud the story the first time. Then read the story again. Pause as you go along, giving children time to use their mats and cards to solve the problems.

Talk About It

✳ How did you decide which set has more?

✳ How can you figure out the difference between two sets of buttons?

Assessment TIPS

- Observe to see that children correctly count out the buttons for each set.

- Check that children are able to determine which set has more or fewer buttons.

- Check that children are able to determine whether two sets of buttons are equal.

Materials (for 2 players)

game directions (page 17)
story mat (page 18)
button cards (page 19)
game spinner (page 20)
brass fastener
paper clip
die

Getting Ready

Copy, cut out, and laminate the game directions and game spinner. Attach the paper clip to the spinner with the brass fastener, as shown on page 5. Use the story mats and button cards that were prepared for the story-mat activity, or prepare additional cards for the game.

Playing the Game

Give each player a story mat and a set of button cards. Place the die and spinner in the center of the table. Then read the directions and model how to play the game. If desired, play it with children the first time. Players can make tally marks on scraps of paper to keep their own score.

The Button Basket

Teddy the Tailor keeps his buttons in a basket. One day, he needed buttons for a coat. He looked in his basket and found 6 round buttons and 5 heart buttons. Did he have more round or more heart buttons?

The next day, Teddy needed 3 leaf buttons for a shirt. He looked in his basket and found 4 leaf buttons and 2 heart buttons. Did he have more leaf or more heart buttons? Teddy took out 3 leaf buttons to sew on the shirt. Does he have more leaf or more heart buttons left in the basket?

Another day, the button basket held 6 leaf buttons and 4 star buttons. Were there fewer leaf or fewer star buttons? Teddy added 2 star buttons to the basket. Does he have fewer star or fewer leaf buttons now?

Yesterday, Teddy put 5 star buttons and 3 round buttons in the basket. Does he have fewer star or fewer round buttons? He used 1 star button on a pair of pants. Now does he have more or fewer star buttons than round buttons?

The Button Basket

Players: 2

How to Play

1. Roll the die. What did it land on? Put that many buttons on your mat.

2. After each player takes a turn, compare the number of buttons on your mats. Do players have the same number of buttons? If so, the round ends.

3. Spin the spinner. Did it land on "more" or on "fewer?"
   - If "more," the player with more buttons earns one point.
   - If "fewer," the player with fewer buttons earns one point.

4. Clear your mats and play again. Keep playing until one player earns 10 points. That player wins the game.

Follow-the-Directions Math Story Mats © 2012 by Ada Goren, Scholastic Teaching Resources

The Button Basket Story Mat

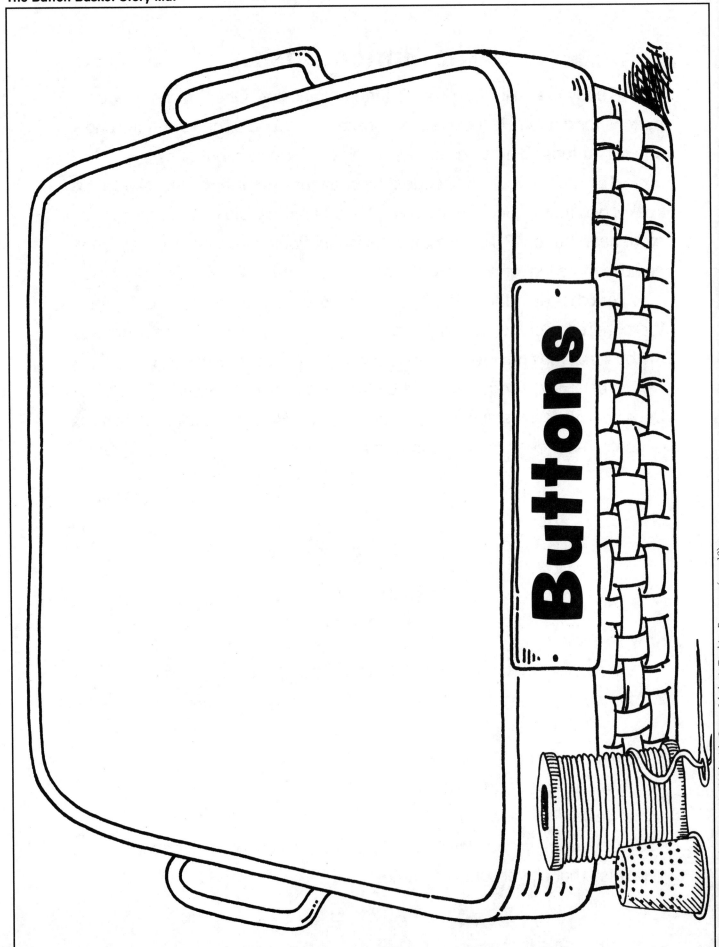

Button Cards

more

fewer

fewer

more

Show Time!

Read-Aloud Story

Materials

read-aloud story (page 22)
story mat (page 23)
animal cards (page 24)

Getting Ready

Copy, color, and cut out a story mat and a set of animal cards for each child in a small group. Laminate the mats and cards for durability.

Using the Story Mat

Give each child a story mat and a set of animal cards. Ask children to listen as you read aloud the story the first time. Then read the story again. Pause as you go along, giving children time to use their mats and cards to solve the problems.

Talk About It

* Why are the animals lined up from left to right?

* What clues in the ordinal numbers helped you decide where in the line to put each animal?

Assessment TIPS

• Check that children are able to place the animals in the correct position on the mat.

• Observe whether children understand the relationship between cardinal and ordinal numbers.

Story-Mat Game

Materials (for 2–4 players)

game directions (page 22)
story mat (page 23)
animal cards (page 24)
game spinner (page 24)
brass fastener
paper clip

Getting Ready

Copy, cut out, and laminate the game directions and game spinner. Attach the paper clip to the spinner with the brass fastener, as shown on page 5. Use the story mats and animal cards that were prepared for the story-mat activity, or prepare additional cards for the game.

Playing the Game

Give each player a story mat and a set of animal cards. Place the spinner in the center of the table. Then read the directions and model how to play the game. If desired, play it with children the first time

Show Time!

The Zaney Zoo animals have been waiting all week for Friday—movie day! Bear got to the theater before the other animals. He was 1st in line. Penguin arrived next. What place in line did Penguin take? The 3rd animal in line was Lion. The next animal in line was Ostrich. What place in line did Ostrich take? Giraffe was running late and was the last animal in line. What place did he take?

The next Friday, Giraffe was at the front of the line. What place in line did he take? The 2nd animal in line was Lion. Bear got in line next. What place did Bear have in the line? The last two animals to arrive were Penguin and Ostrich. Put Penguin in the 4th place in line and Ostrich in the 5th place.

On the next movie day, Ostrich was 1st in line and Bear was 3rd. Giraffe stood between Ostrich and Bear. What place in line did Giraffe take? Penguin was 5th in line. What place in line did Lion take that day?

Story-Mat Game

Show Time!

Players: 2–4

How to Play

1. Choose an animal. Put it in line on any position on your mat.

2. Spin the spinner. What did it land on?

   Is an animal in that position on your mat?

   • If so, your turn ends.

   • If not, choose an animal and place it in that position.

3. Keep taking turns. The first player to fill in all the positions on his or her mat wins the game.

Follow-the-Directions Math Story Mats © 2012 by Ada Goren, Scholastic Teaching Resources

Zany Zoo Theater

Coming Soon...

It's a Jungle Out There!

Now Showing!

Leaping Leopards

Tickets

The line starts here.

Follow-the-Directions Math Story Mats © 2012 by Ada Goren, Scholastic Teaching Resources (page 23)

Animal Cards and Game Spinner

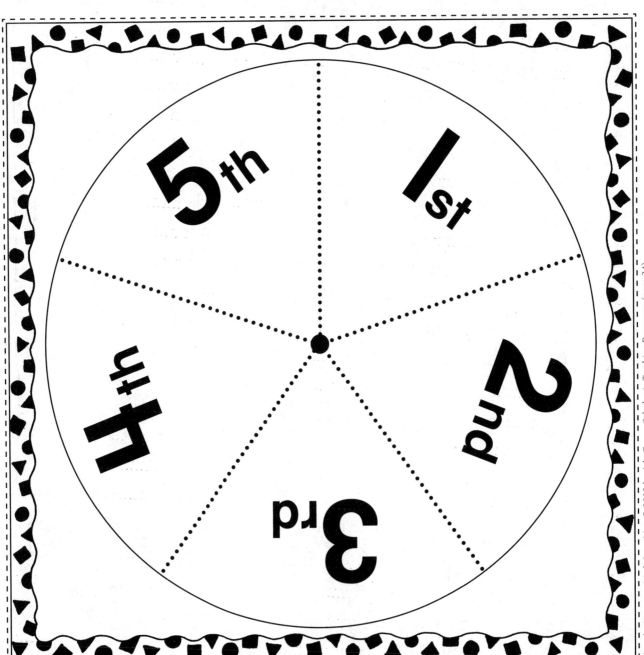

Crow's Corn Cannery

Read-Aloud Story

Materials

read-aloud story (page 26)
story mat (page 27)
canned corn cards (page 28)

Getting Ready

Copy, color, and cut out a story mat and two sets of canned corn cards for each child in a small group. Laminate the mats and cards for durability.

Using the Story Mat

Give each child a story mat and two sets of canned corn cards. Ask children to listen as you read aloud the story the first time. Then read the story again. Pause as you go along, giving children time to use their mats and cards to solve the problems.

Talk About It

* Which of the three orders was the largest?

* How many pallets would you need to fill an order for 500 cans?

* How many cartons would you need to fill an order for 452 cans?

Assessment TIPS

- Observe whether children understand the place-value concepts of hundreds, tens, and ones.

- Check that children grasp the relationship between ones, tens, and hundreds and the role of grouping in place value.

Story-Mat Game

Materials (for 2–4 players)

game directions (page 26)
story mat (page 27)
canned corn cards (page 28)

game spinner (page 29)
brass fastener
paper clip

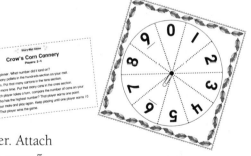

Getting Ready

Copy, cut out, and laminate the game directions and game spinner. Attach the paper clip to the spinner with the brass fastener, as shown on page 5. Use the story mats and corn cards that were prepared for the story-mat activity, or prepare additional cards for the game.

Playing the Game

Give each player a story mat and two sets of canned corn cards. Place the spinner in the center of the table. Then read the directions and model how to play the game. If desired, play it with children the first time. Players can make tally marks on scraps of paper to keep their own score.

25

Crow's Corn Cannery

Crow's Corn Cannery packs corn into single cans. Every 10 cans are packed into a carton. Then every 10 cartons are put on a pallet. Each pallet holds 100 cans of corn.

The first order for 346 cans goes to Cow's General Store. What number is in the hundreds place? Put that many pallets in the hundreds section on the mat. Now, what number is in the tens place? Put that many cartons in the tens section. What number is in the ones place? Put that many cans in the ones section. Great! Move that order off of the mat.

The next order for 623 cans goes to Pig's Fine Foods. Put the number of pallets needed for this order in the hundreds section. How many did you put there? Put the number of cartons and single cans needed in the tens and ones sections. How many did you put in each section? Now, clear the mat.

The last order is for 297 cans. It goes to Raccoon's Restaurant. Put the number of pallets, cartons, and cans for this order on the mat.

Crow's Corn Cannery

Players: 2–4

How to Play

1. Spin the spinner. What number did it land on?
   Put that many pallets in the hundreds section on your mat.

2. Spin again. Put that many cartons in the tens section.

3. Spin one more time. Put that many cans in the ones section.

4. After each player takes a turn, compare the number of cans on your mats. Who has the highest number? That player earns one point.

5. Clear your mats and play again. Keep playing until one player earns 10 points. That player wins the game.

Follow-the-Directions Math Story Mats © 2012 by Ada Goren, Scholastic Teaching Resources

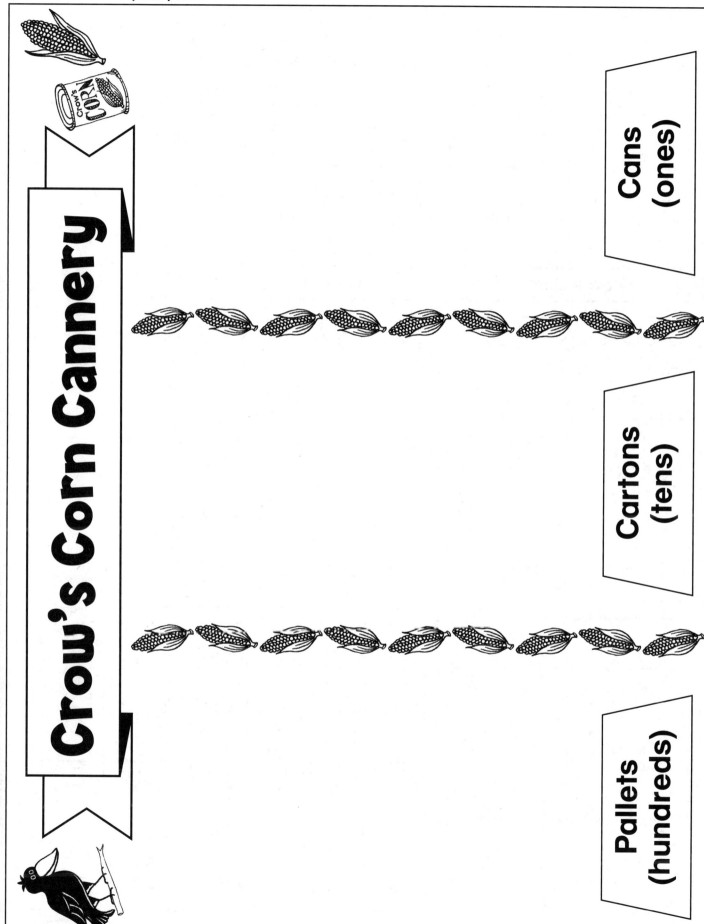

Canned Corn Cards

pallets

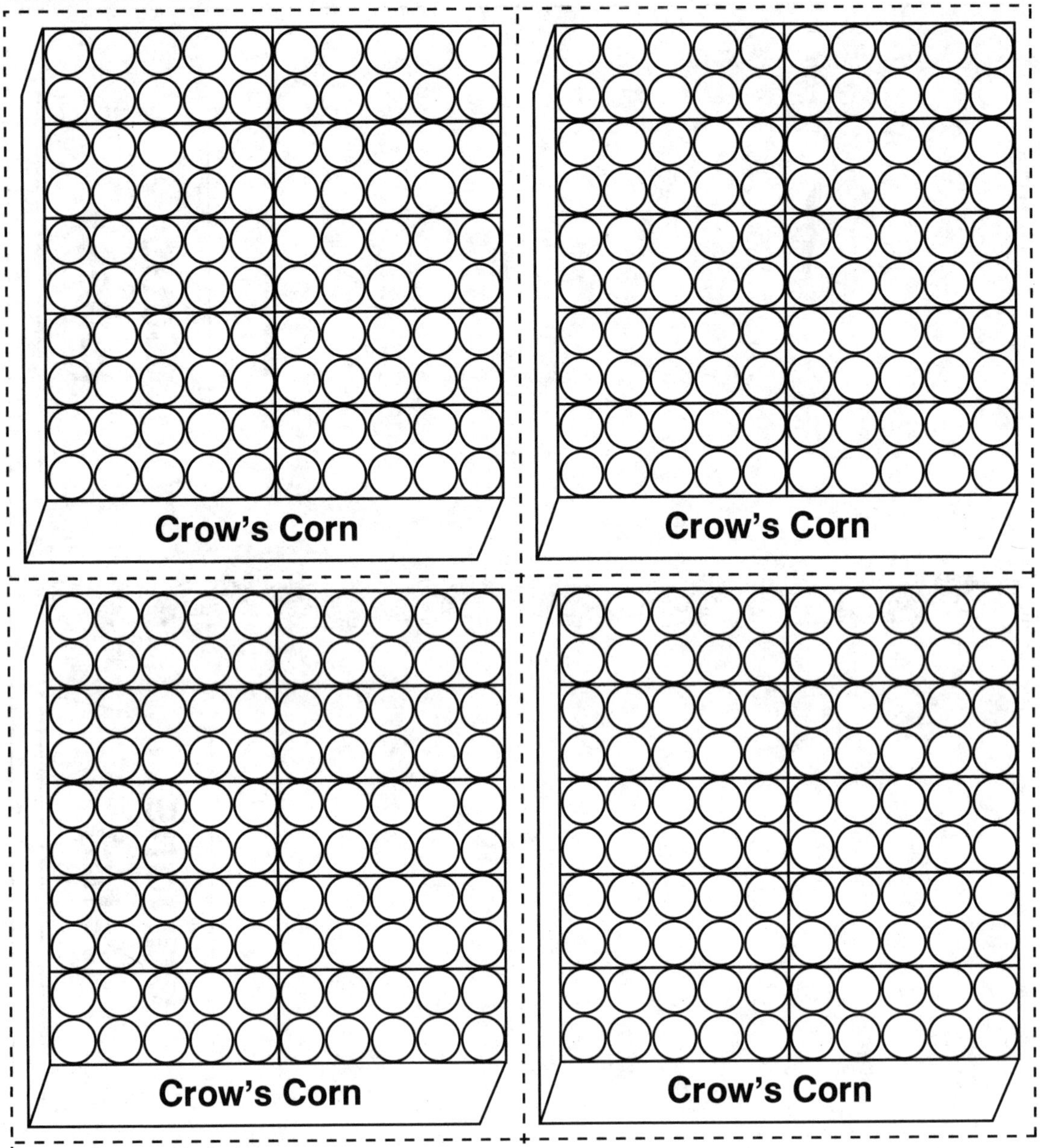

Crow's Corn
Crow's Corn
Crow's Corn
Crow's Corn

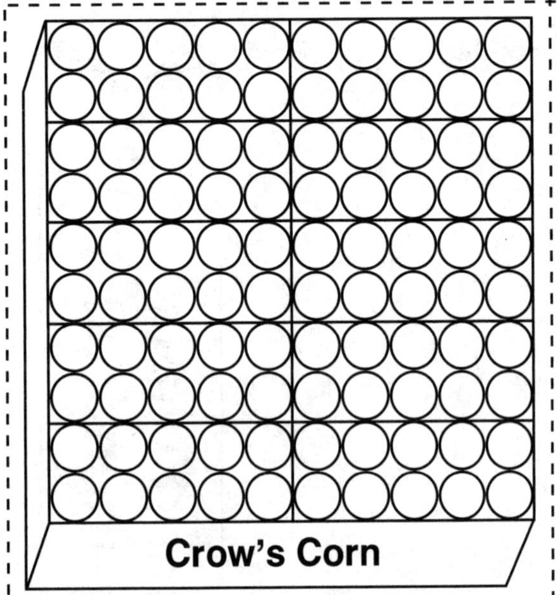

Crow's Corn

cartons

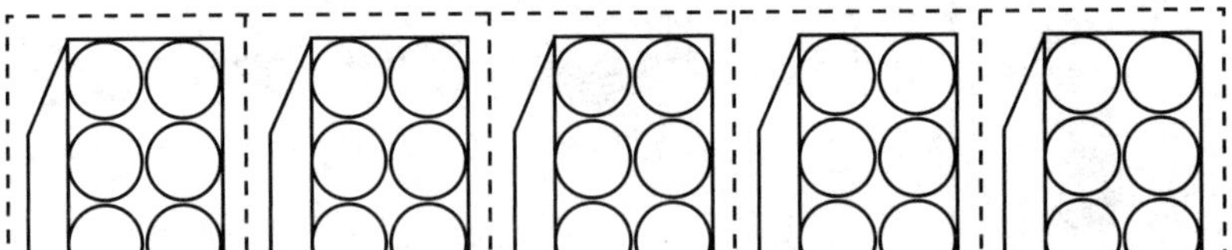

Crow's Corn
Crow's Corn
Crow's Corn
Crow's Corn
Crow's Corn

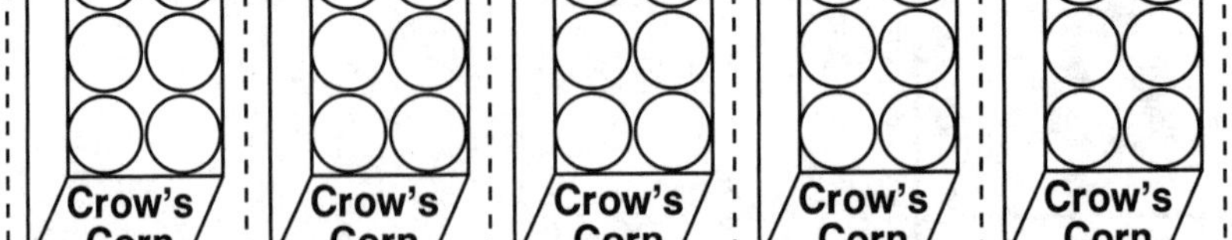

Crow's CORN
Crow's CORN
Crow's CORN
Crow's CORN
Crow's CORN

cans

Game Spinner

Follow-the-Directions Math Story Mats © 2012 by Ada Goren, Scholastic Teaching Resources (page 29)

Lucky Dog!

 Read-Aloud Story

Materials

read-aloud story (page 31)
story mat (page 32)
bone cards (page 33)

Getting Ready

Copy, color, and cut out a copy of the story mat and 12 bone cards for each child in a small group. Laminate the mats and cards for durability.

Using the Story Mat

Give each child a story mat and 12 bone cards. Ask children to listen as you read aloud the story the first time. Then read the story again. Pause as you go along, giving children time to use their mats and cards to solve the problems.

Talk About It

✳ How did you figure out how many bones Lucky had all day?

✳ Imagine Lucky was given 8 bones on Tuesday. Is that more or fewer bones than he got on Monday?

 Story-Mat Game

Materials (for 2–4 players)

game directions (page 31)
story mat (page 32)
bone cards (page 33)
game spinner (page 34)
brass fastener
paper clip

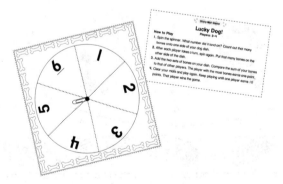

Getting Ready

Copy, cut out, and laminate the game directions and game spinner. Attach the paper clip to the spinner with the brass fastener, as shown on page 5. Use the story mats and bone cards that were prepared for the story-mat activity, or prepare additional cards for the game.

Playing the Game

Give each player a story mat and 12 bone cards. Place the spinner in the center of the table. Then read the directions and model how to play the game. If desired, play it with children the first time. Players can make tally marks on scraps of paper to keep their own score.

Lucky Dog!

It's morning and your dog, Lucky, is ready to eat! Give Lucky 1 bone before you go to school. Put that bone on the dog dish. When school ends, you hurry home to see Lucky. He barks "Hello!" and wags his tail as soon as he sees you. Then Lucky runs to his dish to look for more bones. Give Lucky 2 bones. How many bones did Lucky get so far today? Set those bones aside.

After your family has dinner, Mom tells you that Lucky looks hungry. Give Lucky 3 more bones. Put them on the dog dish. Just before bedtime, Dad asks you to give Lucky a bone for the night. Put 1 more bone on Lucky's dish. How many bones did Lucky get after dinner?

While you get ready for bed, you wonder how many bones in all Lucky had today. Count all the bones you gave Lucky. How many did he have? (Don't forget to count the bones you set aside earlier!)

✦ **Story-Mat Game** ✦

Lucky Dog!

Players: 2–4

How to Play

1. Spin the spinner. What number did it land on? Count out that many bones onto one side of your dog dish.

2. After each player takes a turn, spin again. Put that many bones on the other side of the dish.

3. Add the two sets of bones on your dish. Compare the sum of your bones to that of other players. The player with the most bones earns one point.

4. Clear your mats and play again. Keep playing until one player earns 10 points. That player wins the game.

Follow-the-Directions Math Story Mats © 2012 by Ada Goren, Scholastic Teaching Resources

Lucky Dog! Story Mat

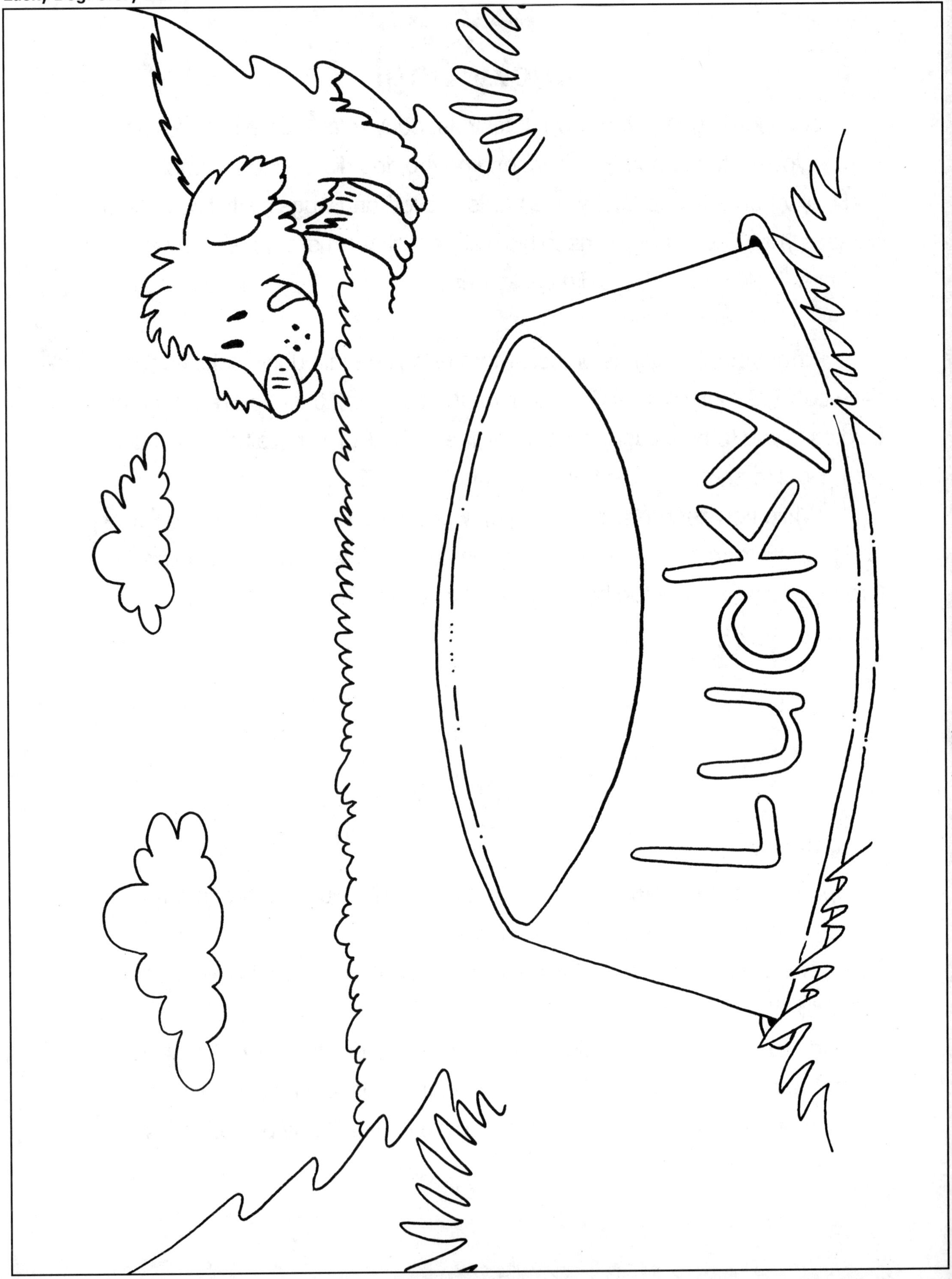

Bone Cards

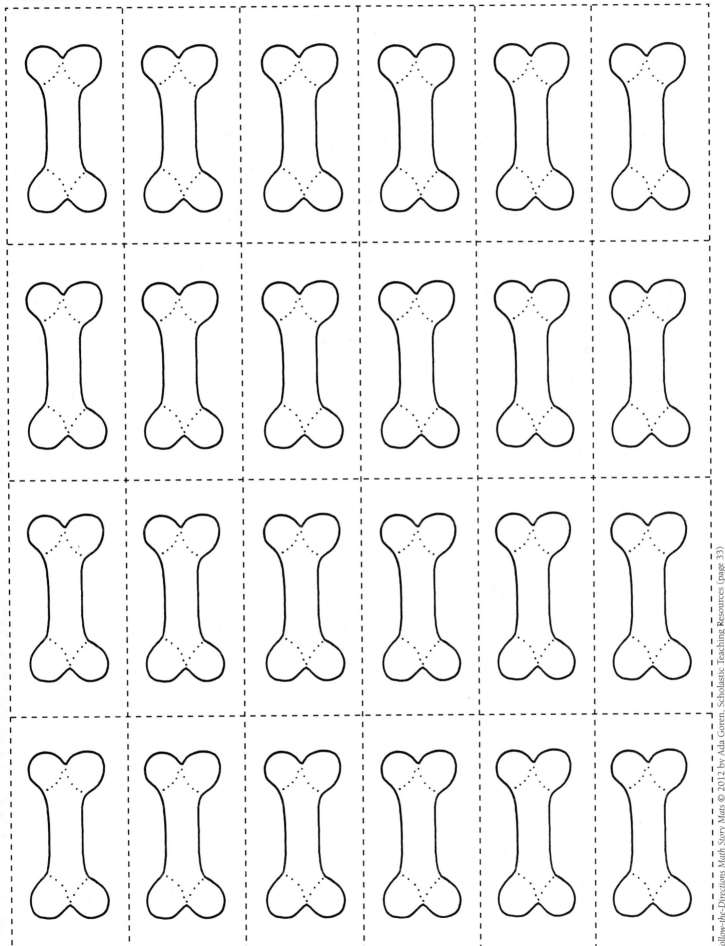

Game Spinner

Follow-the-Directions Math Story Mats © 2012 by Ada Goren, Scholastic Teaching Resources (page 34)

Finn's Fish

Read-Aloud Story

Materials

read-aloud story (page 36)
story mat (page 37)
fish cards (page 38)

Getting Ready

Copy, color, and cut out a story mat and two sets of fish cards for each child in a small group. Laminate the mats and cards for durability.

Using the Story Mat

Give each child a story mat and two sets of fish cards. Ask children to listen as you read aloud the story the first time. Then read the story again. Pause as you go along, giving children time to use their mats and cards to solve the problems.

Talk About It

❋ How did you figure out how many fish were in each boy's tank?

❋ Imagine Finn has 12 fish in his tank. How many more fish does he need to have 17 fish?

❋ If Marco has 6 striped fish and the same number of spotted fish, how many fish does he have in all?

Assessment TIPS

- Check for children's ability to count out the correct number of fish.

- Observe if children "count on" to find the sum of their sets.

- For the game, check that children accurately count out each set of fish, then correctly add the sets together. Also, observe whether they correctly compare the number of fish and identify the mat with the most fish.

Story-Mat Game

Materials (for 2–4 players)

game directions (page 36)
story mat (page 37)
fish cards (page 38)
game spinner (page 39)
brass fastener
paper clip

Getting Ready

Copy, cut out, and laminate the game directions and game spinner. Attach the paper clip to the spinner with the brass fastener, as shown on page 5. Use the story mats and fish cards that were prepared for the story-mat activity, or prepare additional cards for the game.

Playing the Game

Give each player a story mat and a set of fish cards. Place the spinner in the center of the table. Then read the directions and model how to play the game. If desired, play it with children the first time. Players can make tally marks on scraps of paper to keep their own score.

Finn's Fish

Finn is very proud of his tank full of tropical fish! He has 7 spotted fish and 4 striped fish. How many fish does he have? Finn's friend Marco brings him 2 more striped fish as a gift. How many striped fish does Finn have now? How many fish does he have in all? Clear the fish off of the mat.

Finn helps Marco set up his own fish tank. Together, they buy 9 plain fish at the pet store. Then Marco's mom surprises him with 6 spotted fish. How many fish does Marco have? Later, Finn gives Marco 3 spotted fish for his birthday. How many spotted fish does Marco have now? How many fish does he have in all? Clear the mat.

Finn and Marco go to the pet store to look at the fish there. Finn counted 8 striped fish in a tank. Marco counted 5 spotted fish in the same tank. How many fish are in the tank? The store clerk put 2 more spotted fish in the tank. Now, how many fish are there?

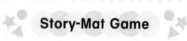

Story-Mat Game

Finn's Fish

Players: 2–4

How to Play

1. Spin the spinner. What number did it land on? Count out that many fish onto one side of your mat.

2. After each player takes a turn, spin again. Put that many fish on the other side of your mat.

3. Add the two sets of fish on your mat. Compare the sum of your fish to that of other players. The player with the most fish earns one point.

4. Clear your mats and play again. Keep playing until one player earns 10 points. That player wins the game.

Follow-the-Directions Math Story Mats © 2012 by Ada Goren, Scholastic Teaching Resources

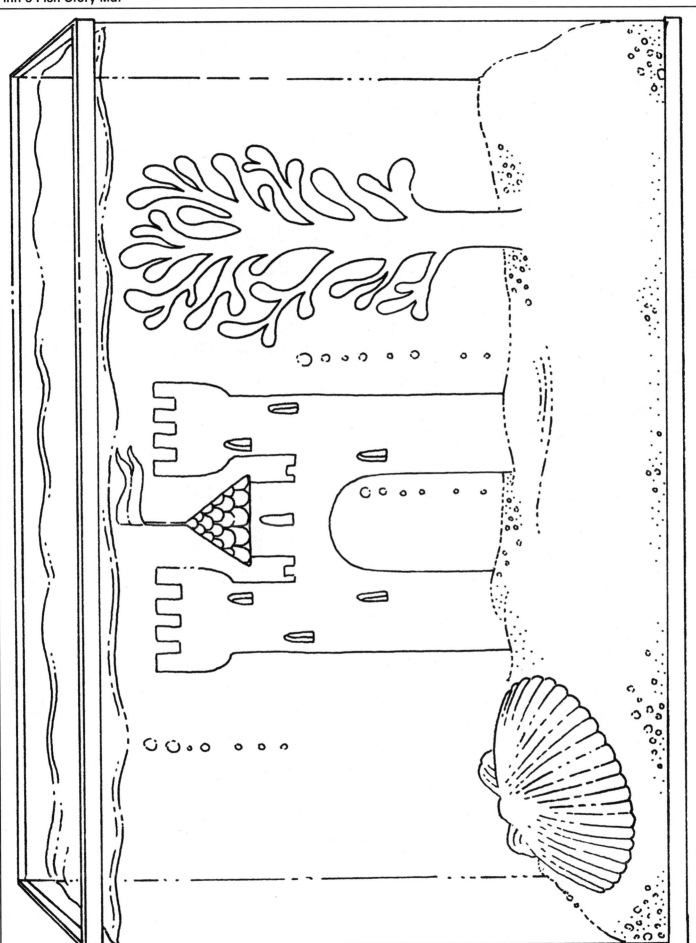

Fish Cards

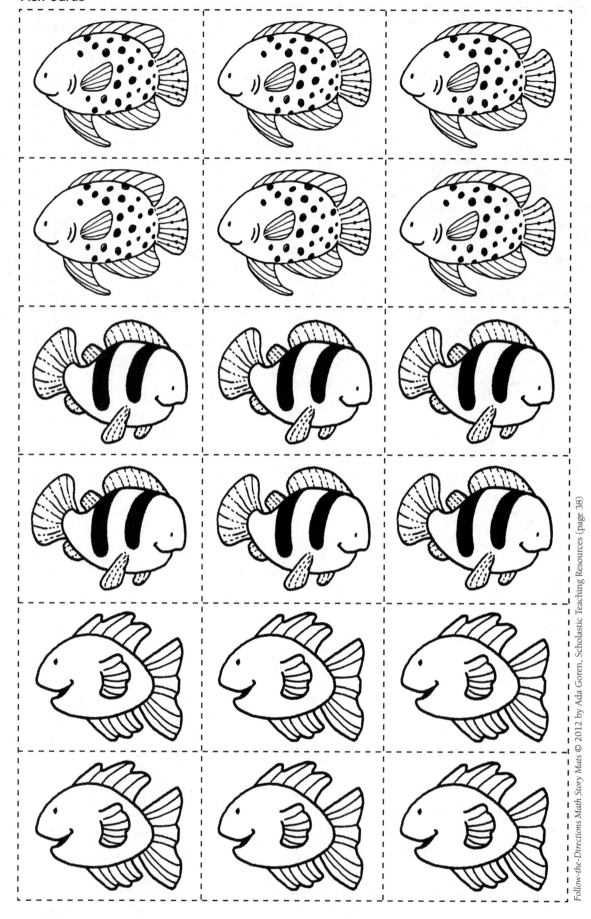

Game Spinner

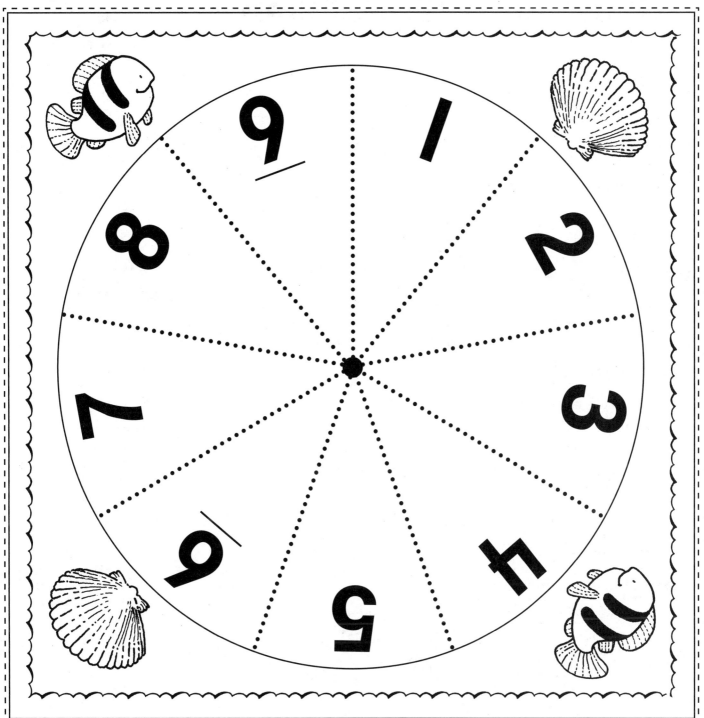

Squirrelly Subtraction

Materials

read-aloud story (page 41)
story mat (page 42)
acorn cards (page 43)

Getting Ready

Copy, color, and laminate a copy of the story mat and ten acorn cards
for each child. Laminate the mats and cards for durability.

Using the Story Mat

Give each child a story mat and ten acorn cards. Ask children to listen as you
read aloud the story the first time. Then read the story again. Pause as you go
along, giving children time to use their mats and cards to solve the problems.

Talk About It

❋ How did you figure out how many acorns were left each time some were
taken away?

❋ If Sam has 9 acorns and he gives 5 to Sally, how many will he have left?

❋ Imagine there are 7 acorns in a tree and 4 fall to the ground. How many
acorns will be left in the tree?

 Story-Mat Game

Assessment TIPS

• Check that children
count out their acorns
correctly.

• Observe if children
"count back" to find the
differences.

• Check for children's
accuracy in subtracting
to solve the problems.

• For the game, determine
if children easily
verbalize the subtraction
problems.

Materials (for 2–4 players)

game directions (page 41)
story mat (page 42)
acorn cards (page 43)
number cube (page 44)
glue

Getting Ready

Copy, cut out, and laminate the game directions and number cube. Assemble the
number cube as shown on page 5. Use the story mats and acorn cards that were
prepared for the story-mat activity, or prepare additional cards for the game.

Playing the Game

Give each player a story mat and ten acorn cards. Place the number cube in the
center of the table. Then read the directions and model how to play the game.
If desired, play it with children the first time. Players can make tally marks on
scraps of paper to keep their own score.

Squirrelly Subtraction

It's a beautiful day! Sam and Sally Squirrel go out to gather acorns in the park. Put 10 acorns on the ground on the mat. First, Sam comes along and picks up 2 acorns. Take those acorns off of the mat. How many are left? Next, Sally comes by and takes 4 acorns. Take away those acorns. Now how many are left? Later, Sam runs by and takes 1 more acorn. Take away that acorn. How many acorns are left on the mat? Clear the acorns off of the mat.

The next day, 9 acorns fell to the ground. Put that number of acorns on the mat. Sally starts hunting first. She carries 3 acorns back to her nest. Take away those acorns. How many acorns are left? Soon, Sam comes by and takes 3 acorns. Take those acorns off of the mat. How many are there now? Then Sam and Sally come back together. Each squirrel takes 1 acorn. Take away those acorns. How many acorns are left on the mat?

Squirrelly Subtraction

Players: 2–4

How to Play

1. Put your acorns on the mat between the trees.

2. Roll the number cube. What number did it land on? Take that many acorns off of the mat. How many acorns are left?

3. Say the number sentence for the subtraction problem you just solved. For example: *10 – 3 = 7.*

4. Players keep taking turns. The first player to remove all the acorns from his or her mat—on an exact roll of the number cube—earns 1 point.

5. Clear your mats and play again. Keep playing until one player earns 5 points. That player wins the game.

Follow-the-Directions Math Story Mats © 2012 by Ada Goren, Scholastic Teaching Resources

Squirrelly Subtraction Story Mat

Acorn Cards

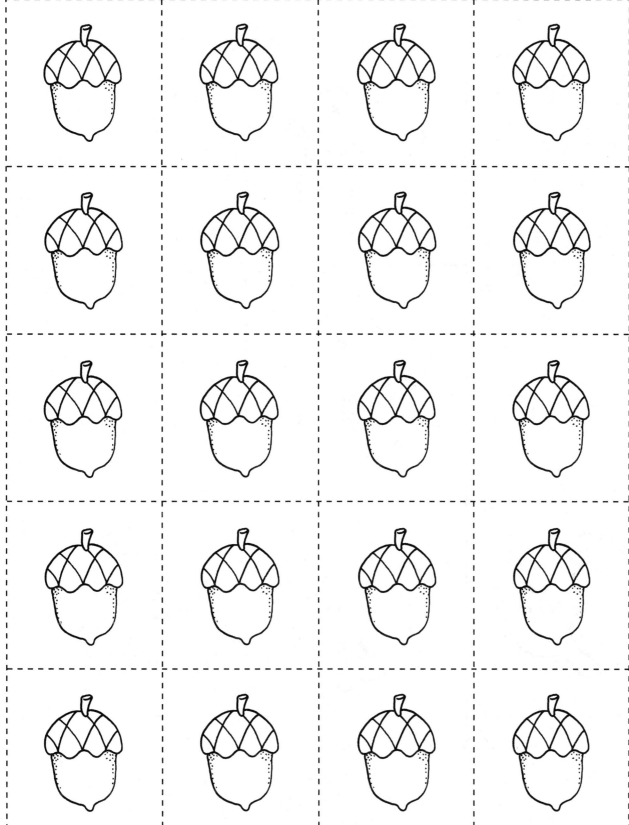

Follow-the-Directions Math Story Mats © 2012 by Ada Go·ren, Scholastic Teaching Resources (page 43)

Number Cube

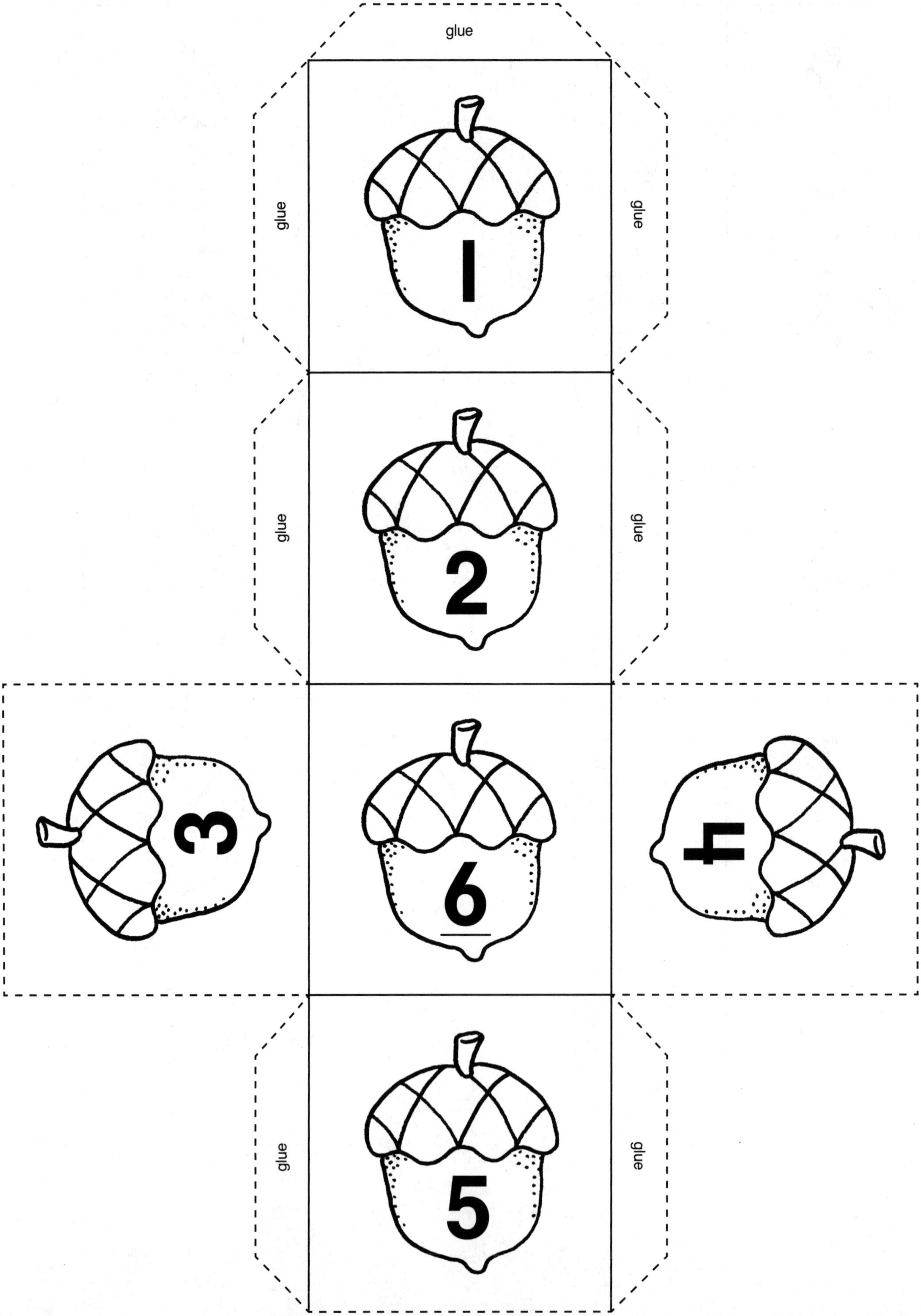

glue

glue

glue

glue

glue

glue

1

2

3

6

4

5

Follow-the-Directions Math Story Mats © 2012 by Ada Goren, Scholastic Teaching Resources (page 44)

Shells on the Sand

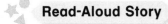
Read-Aloud Story

Materials

read-aloud story (page 46)
story mat (page 47)
shell cards (page 48)

Getting Ready

Copy, color, and cut out a copy of the story mat and a set of shell cards
for each child in a small group. Laminate the mats and cards for durability.

Using the Story Mat

Give each child a story mat and a set of shell cards. Ask children to listen as you
read aloud the story the first time. Then read the story again. Pause as you go
along, giving children time to use their mats and cards to solve the problems.

Talk About It

✳ How did you figure out how many shells were left each time some were
taken away?

✳ If you have 17 shells and your little sister has 13, who has more shells?
How many more?

Assessment TIPS

- Check that children count out their shells correctly.

- Observe if children "count back" to find the differences.

- Check for children's accuracy in subtracting to solve the problems.

- For the game, determine if children easily verbalize the subtraction problems.

Story-Mat Game

Materials (for 2–4 players)

game directions (page 46)   game spinner (page 49)
story mat (page 47)   brass fastener
shell cards (page 48)   paper clip
number cards (page 49)   paper bag

Getting Ready

Copy, cut out, and laminate the game directions, number cards, and game spinner.
Attach the paper clip to the spinner with the brass fastener, as shown on page 5.
Use the story mats and shell cards that were prepared for the story-mat activity, or prepare
additional cards for the game.

Playing the Game

Give each player a story mat and a set of shell cards. Put the number cards in the paper
bag. Place the bag and the spinner in the center of the table. Then read the directions and
model how to play the game. If desired, play it with children the first time. Players can
make tally marks on scraps of paper to keep their own score.

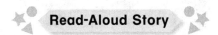

Shells on the Sand

Ahhh! Your family is finally on vacation at the beach! It's time to look for shells. Soon, you've found 18 shells. Put those shells on the mat. Oh, no! A big wave just washed away 6 shells! Take away those shells. How many shells do you have now? Your little sister comes along and takes 5 shells for a necklace. Take away those shells. How many shells are left? Give 4 shells to a friend who passes by. Now how many shells are there? Clear the shells off of the mat.

The next day, you find 15 shells. Put that number of shells on the mat. Your mom takes a walk and sees the shells. She picks up 4 shells and puts them in her pocket. Take away those shells. How many are left? Your two brothers come by and pick out 3 shells each. Take those shells off of the mat. How many shells are left now? As the tide comes in, 4 shells get washed away. Take away those shells. How many shells are left on the mat?

Shells on the Sand

Players: 2–4

How to Play

1. Take a number card out of the bag. Put that many shells on your mat.

2. Spin the spinner. What number did it land on? Take that many shells off of your mat. How many shells are left?

3. Say the number sentence for the subtraction problem you just solved. For example: $13 - 2 = 11$. Put the number card back in the bag.

4. Players keep taking turns. The first player to remove all the shells from his or her mat—on an exact spin—earns 1 point.

5. Clear your mats and play again. Keep playing until one player earns 5 points. That player wins the game.

Follow-the-Directions Math Story Mats © 2012 by Ada Goren, Scholastic Teaching Resources

Shells on the Sand Story Mat

Shell Cards

Game Spinner and Number Cards

13	14	15
16	17	18

The Vegetable Garden

 Read-Aloud Story

Materials

read-aloud story (page 51)
story mat (page 52)

divider strips (page 53)
vegetable cards (page 54)

Getting Ready

Copy, color, and cut out a copy of the story mat and two sets of vegetable cards for each child in a small group. Also, copy and laminate a set of divider strips for each child. Laminate the mats, cards, and divider strips for durability. If desired, have children use removable adhesive to hold the divider strips in place on their mat.

Using the Story Mat

Give each child a story mat, two sets of vegetable cards, and a set of divider strips. Ask children to listen as you read aloud the story the first time. Reread the story, and show children how to use the divider strips to divide the garden as indicated in the story. Then read the story again. Pause as you go along, giving children time to use their mats, cards, and divider strips to solve the problems.

Talk About It

✳ If the garden is divided into eight equal parts, and only five parts are planted with peas, what fraction of the garden does not have peas?

✳ Show how you can divide the garden into three equal parts. What fraction would one part of that garden be called?

 Story-Mat Game

Materials (for 2–4 players)

game directions (page 51)
story mat (page 52)
divider strips (page 53)

fraction cards (page 53)
vegetable cards (page 54)
paper bag

Getting Ready

Copy, cut out, and laminate the game directions and fraction cards. Use the story mats, divider strips, and vegetable cards that were prepared for the story-mat activity, or prepare additional cards for the game. If desired, have children use removable adhesive to hold the divider strips in place on their mat.

Playing the Game

Give each player a story mat and one set of the vegetable cards and divider strips. Put the fraction cards in the paper bag. Place the bag in the center of the table. Then read the directions and model how to play the game. If desired, play it with children the first time. Players can make tally marks on scraps of paper to keep their own score.

The Vegetable Garden

Gabby Gardner wants to plant carrots in one half of her garden and lettuce in the other half. Help Gabby divide her garden and plant the vegetables. Now, clear the mat.

Garrett Gardner plans to plant broccoli, carrots, squash, and tomatoes, each in an equal part of his garden. Help Garrett divide his garden and plant the vegetables. What fraction of the garden has tomatoes? What fraction has broccoli? Clear the mat.

The Gardner twins, Gloria and Glenda, want to grow a garden together. Each girl will plant half of the garden. Both girls decided to divide their half into four equal parts. Help them divide the garden. How many equal parts are there? Gloria planted onions, corn, squash, and lettuce in her parts of the garden. Glenda planted peas, squash, carrots, and onions in her parts. Help the twins plant the garden. What fraction of the garden has onions? What fraction has peas? What fraction is used for corn and squash?

Story-Mat Game

The Vegetable Garden
Players: 2–4

How to Play

1. Use the divider strips to divide your garden into eight equal sections.

2. Take a card out of the bag. What fraction is on the card?

3. Put enough vegetable cards on your mat to cover that fraction of the garden. Put the fraction card back in the bag.

4. Players keep taking turns. The first player to cover all the sections of his or her mat—on an exact count—earns 1 point.

5. Clear your mats and play again. Keep playing until one player earns 5 points. That player wins the game.

Follow-the-Directions Math Story Mats © 2012 by Ada Goren, Scholastic Teaching Resources

The Vegetable Garden Story Mat

Divider Strips and Fraction Cards

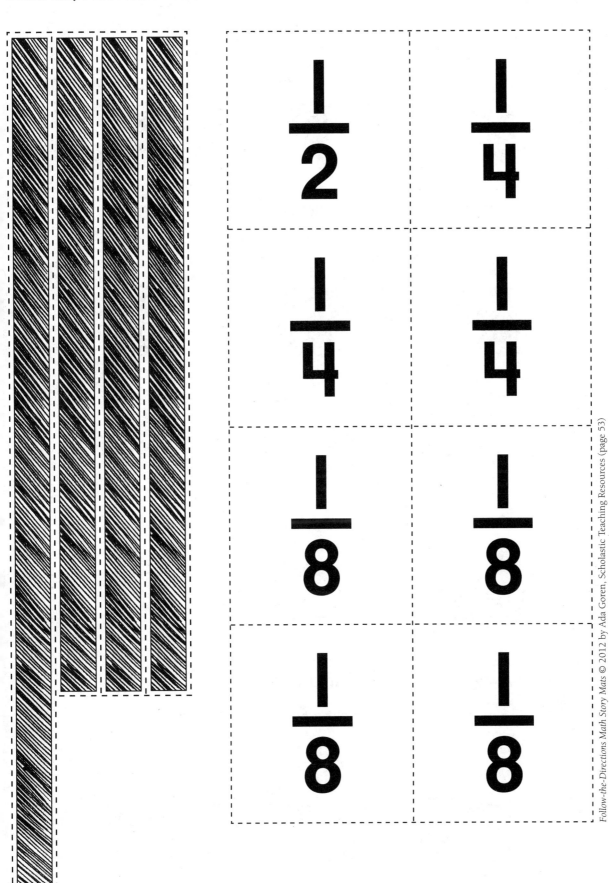

Follow-the-Directions Math Story Mats © 2012 by Ada Goren, Scholastic Teaching Resources (page 53)

Vegetable Cards

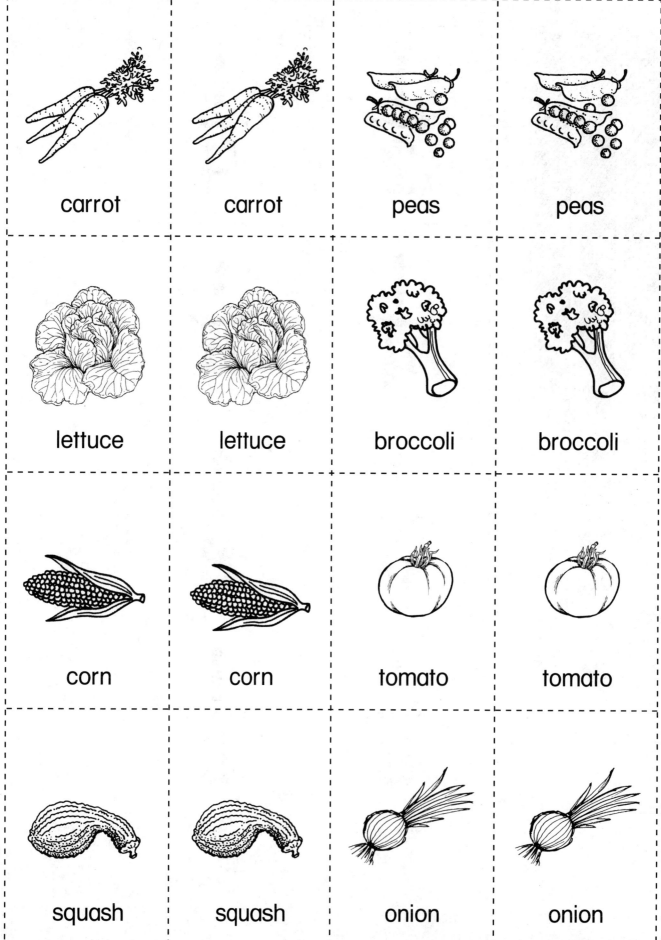

carrot	carrot	peas	peas
lettuce	lettuce	broccoli	broccoli
corn	corn	tomato	tomato
squash	squash	onion	onion

Fabulous Fair Treats!

Materials

read-aloud story (page 56)
story mat (page 57)
coin cards (page 58)

Getting Ready

Copy, color, and cut out a copy of the story mat and a set of coin cards for each child in a small group. Laminate the mats and cards for durability.

Using the Story Mat

Give each child a story mat and a set of coin cards. Have children pile their coin cards near the top of their mat. Then ask them to listen as you read aloud the story the first time. Read the story again. Pause as you go along, giving children time to use their mats and cards to solve the problems.

Talk About It

* How did you know how much money you had?

* Could you buy any treats with one dime? Why not?

* Which item cost the most? Which one cost the least?

Assessment TIPS

- Check that children know the value of each of these coins: nickel, dime, and quarter.

- Determine whether children can count out and match coin combinations to the costs of the items.

- Check that children are able to add the value of their coins accurately.

Story-Mat Game

Materials (for 2–4 players)

game directions (page 56)
story mat (page 57)
coin cards (page 58)
coin cube (page 59)
glue
plastic chips (four per player)

Getting Ready

Copy, cut out, and laminate the game directions and coin cube. Assemble the coin cube as shown on page 5. Use the story mats and coin cards that were prepared for the story-mat activity, or prepare additional cards for the game.

Playing the Game

Give each player a story mat and four plastic chips (to use as game markers). Place the coin cube and cards in the center of the table. Then read the directions and model how to play the game. If desired, play it with children the first time.

Fabulous Fair Treats!

Hooray! It's fair time, and you have 2 quarters, 3 dimes, and 5 nickels to spend! Take those coins from your pile. How much money do you have?

You decide to get cotton candy. Which coins can you use to buy it? Place those coins on the treat. How much money do you have left?

Later, you decide to get popcorn. Which coins can you use to buy the treat? Put those coins on the popcorn. Now how much money do you have? Do you have enough to buy something else? If so, put those coins on the treat you want to buy. Clear the coins off of the mat.

Oh, boy! Mom gives you another quarter and dime. Take those coins from the pile and put them with the rest of your money. How much do you have now? Chose two treats that you can afford to buy. What did you choose and how much does each cost? Put the money for each treat on its picture. Do you have any money left? If so, how much?

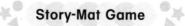

Story-Mat Game

Fabulous Fair Treats!

Players: 2–4

How to Play

1. Put a game marker on each treat on your mat.

2. Roll the coin cube. What did it land on? Take that coin card from the pile.

3. Keep taking turns. Count your money at the end of each turn.

4. Do you have exactly enough to buy a treat? If so, take the marker off of that treat. Put those coins back in the pile.

5. Keep playing, collecting coins until you have exactly enough money to buy a treat marked with a game marker. The first player to buy all of his or her treats wins the game.

Follow-the-Directions Math Story Mats © 2012 by Ada Goren, Scholastic Teaching Resources

Fabulous Fair Treats!

Frozen Lemonade

50¢

Cotton Candy

30¢

Candy Apple

20¢

Popcorn

40¢

Coin Cards

Coin Cube

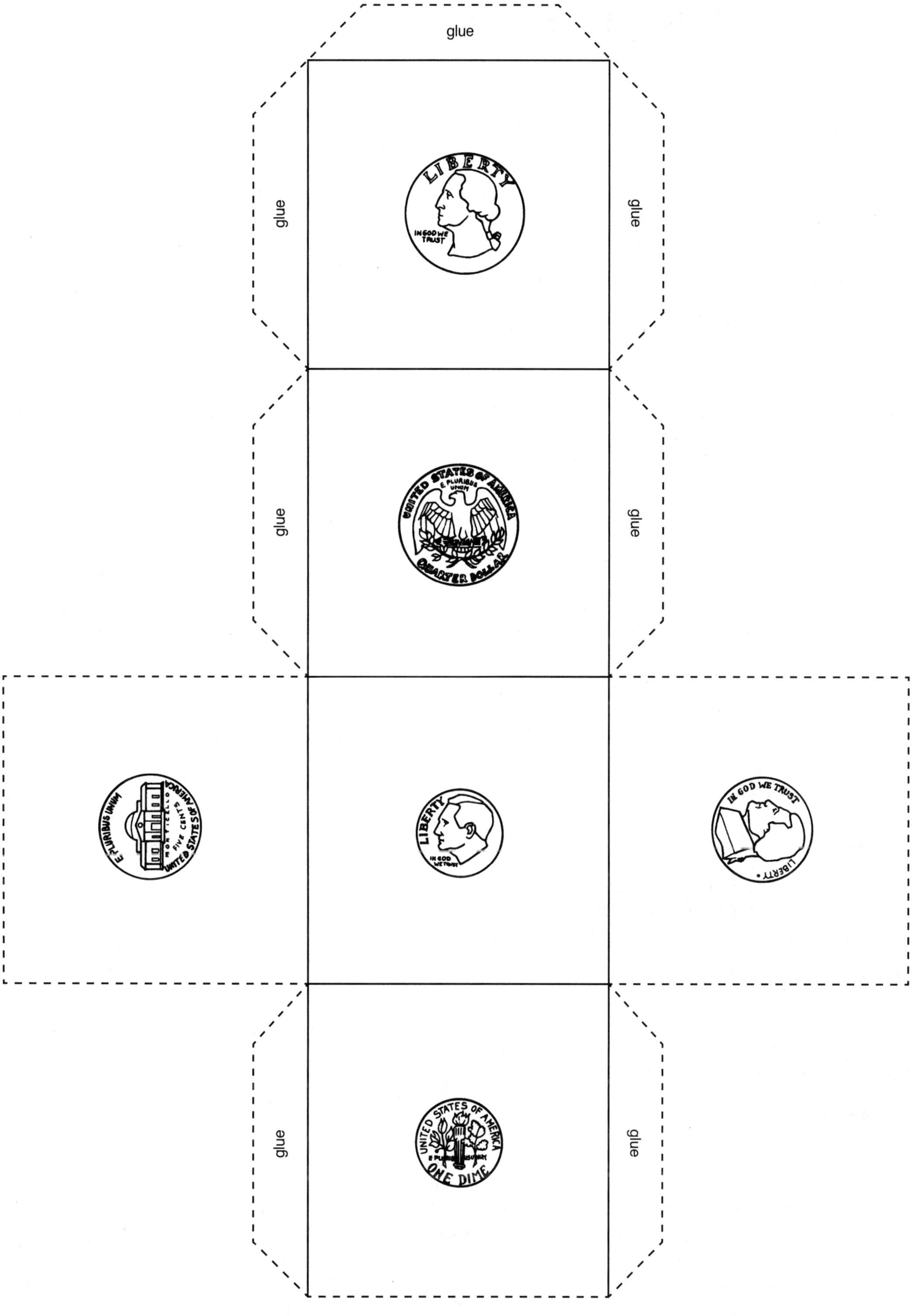
glue
glue
glue
LIBERTY
IN GOD WE TRUST
glue
glue
UNITED STATES OF AMERICA
E PLURIBUS UNUM
QUARTER DOLLAR
E PLURIBUS UNUM
MONTICELLO
FIVE CENTS
UNITED STATES OF AMERICA
LIBERTY
IN GOD WE TRUST
IN GOD WE TRUST
LIBERTY
glue
glue
UNITED STATES OF AMERICA
E PLURIBUS UNUM
ONE DIME

Dragon's Day

Read-Aloud Story

Materials

read-aloud story (page 61)
story mat (page 62)
clock hands (page 63)
brass fastener

Getting Ready

Copy, color, and cut out a story mat and a set of clock hands for each child in a small group. Laminate the pieces for durability. Then use the brass fastener to attach the clock hands to each clock where indicated.

Using the Story Mat

Give each child a story-mat clock. Ask children to listen as you read aloud the story the first time. Then read the story again. Pause as you go along, giving children time to use their assembled story-mat clocks and cards to solve the problems.

Talk About It

* What did you notice about how the hands moved around the clock as Dragon's day went on?

* If Dragon goes to bed at 9:00 tomorrow night, will that time be earlier or later than the time he went to bed tonight?

Assessment TIPS

• Check that children accurately read the times on their cards.

• Observe if children correctly set their clocks to match the named or printed time.

• Determine if children grasp the concepts of "earlier" and "later" as applied to the time measured by clocks.

Story-Mat Game

Materials (for 2 players)

game directions (page 61)
assembled story-mat clock
activity cards (page 63)

game spinner (page 64)
brass fastener
paper clip

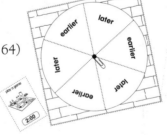

Getting Ready

Copy, cut out, and laminate the game directions, activity cards, and game spinner. Attach the paper clip to the spinner with the brass fastener, as shown on page 5. Use the story-mat clocks that were prepared for the story-mat activity to play the game.

Playing the Game

Give each player a story-mat clock. Shuffle the activity cards and stack them facedown. Place the stack of cards and the spinner in the center of the table. Then read the directions and model how to play the game. If desired, play it with children the first time. Players can make tally marks on scraps of paper to keep their own score.

Dragon's Day

Dragon has a busy day today! Help Dragon follow his schedule by setting your clock to the correct time for each of his activities.

Dragon gets out of bed at 7:00 in the morning. He washes up, dresses, and eats breakfast. At 8:30, he heads out to catch the bus.

His fire-breathing class starts at 9:00. Dragon really enjoys this class! At 10:30, he gets his scales polished. He returns home for lunch at 12:30.

After lunch and a quick nap, Dragon goes to the dentist for a 2:00 tooth-sharpening appointment. He gets home at 3:00, just in time to see his favorite TV show—*Castle Crashers*. Then he heads out at 4:00 to meet his friends at the Zig-Zaggin' Dragon Game Room.

Dragon spends two hours with his friends. At 6:00, he hurries home to make dinner. Then he takes a hot bubble bath at 7:30. Dragon picks up a book to read at 8:30. After a busy day, Dragon curls up in his bed at 10:00 to go to sleep.

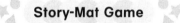

Dragon's Day

Players: 2

How to Play

1. Take an activity card from the stack. Read the activity.

What time does it start? Set your clock to that time.

2. After players set their clocks, compare the times.

Who has the earlier time? Who has the later time?

3. Spin the spinner. Did it land on "earlier" or "later?"

• If "earlier," the player with the earlier time earns one point.

• If "later," the player with the later time earns one point.

4. Keep playing until one player earns 10 points. That player wins the game.

Follow-the-Directions Math Story Mats © 2012 by Ada Goren, Scholastic Teaching Resources

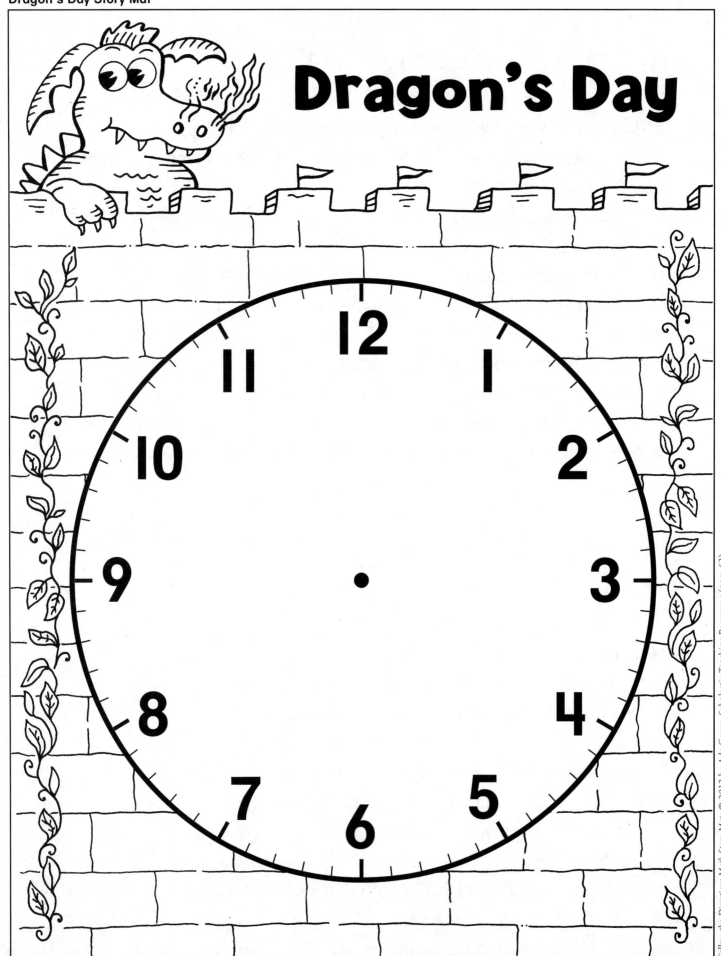

Dragon's Day

Activity Cards and Clock Hands

eat lunch	take a nap	play a game	jump rope
12:30	**1:30**	**2:00**	**2:30**
play ball	do a puzzle	use the computer	eat supper
3:00	**4:30**	**5:00**	**6:30**
take a bath	brush teeth	read a book	go to bed
7:30	**8:00**	**9:00**	**10:00**

Game Spinner

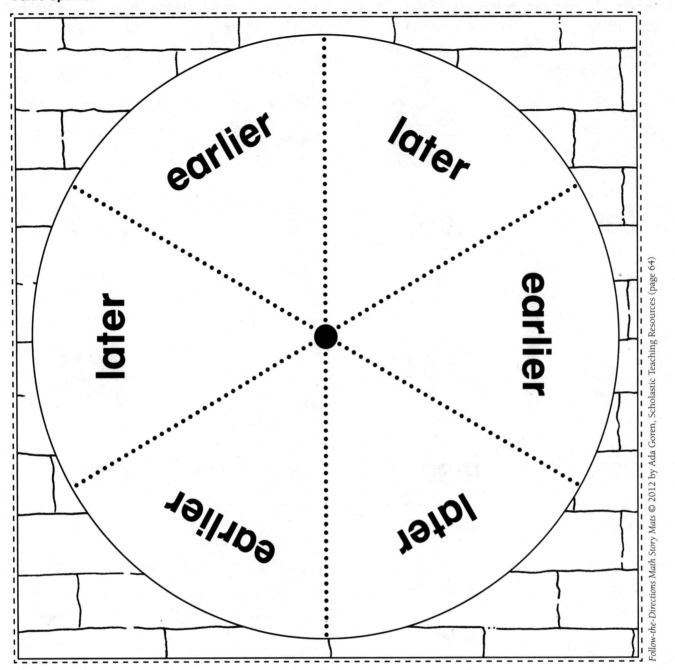

Cat's Calendar

Read-Aloud Story

Materials

read-aloud story (page 66)
story mat (page 67)
calendar cards (page 68)

Getting Ready

Copy, color, and cut out a story mat and a set of calendar cards for each child in a small group. Laminate the pieces for durability. If desired, have children use removable adhesive to hold the calendar cards in place on their mat.

Using the Story Mat

Give each child a story mat and a set of calendar cards. Ask children to listen as you read aloud the story the first time. Then read the story again. Pause as you go along, giving children time to use their story mats and cards to solve the problems.

Talk About It

❋ How can you tell which day of the week each date falls on?

❋ Two of Chester's activities fall on the same day of the week. Which activities are they? On which day of the week do they occur?

Assessment TIPS

- Observe if children correctly identify the days of the week and the dates on the calendar.

- During the game, determine whether children correctly read the day-of-the week cards.

- During the game, check that children can locate their specific day and the different numbers on the calendar.

Story-Mat Game

Materials (for 2–4 players)

game directions (page 66)   brass fastener
story mat (page 67)   paper clip
day-of-the week cards (page 68)   paper bag
game spinner (page 68)   crayons

Getting Ready

Copy, cut out, and laminate the game directions, day-of-the week cards, and game spinner. Also, copy a story mat for each player. Then attach the paper clip to the spinner with the brass fastener, as shown on page 5.

Playing the Game

Give each player a story mat and crayons. Put the day-of-the week cards in the paper bag. Place the bag and the spinner in the center of the table. Then read the directions and model how to play the game. If desired, play it with children the first time.

Cat's Calendar

Chester Cat will be very busy this month! Help him mark his calendar with the special things he has going on, so he doesn't forget them.

He has a grooming appointment on the 5th. Put the brush on that date. Chester will leave for a two-day fishing trip on the 10th. Put the fish on that date. On the 14th, Chester will go to Cousin Fluffy's birthday party. Put the birthday cake on that date. How many days are between his grooming appointment and the birthday party?

On the 25th, Chester will go with his best friend, Midnight, to a catnip-tasting buffet at the Cool Kitty Café. Put the dish of cat food on that date. He plans to go to a yarn sale on the 28th. Put the yarn on that date. How many days after his fishing trip will Chester go to the Cool Kitty Café? Will Chester go to the birthday party before or after his fishing trip? Is the yarn sale closer to the beginning of the month or the end of the month?

Story-Mat Game

Cat's Calendar
Players: 2–4

How to Play

1. Take a card out of the bag and read it. Find the column for that day on your mat. This will be your column. Then color a free space in your column:
   - For Sunday, Monday, Friday, or Saturday, color the empty square in that column.
   - For Tuesday, Wednesday, or Thursday, color any square in that column.
2. Spin the spinner. What number did it land on? Is that number on any of your squares? If so, color one of those squares.
3. Players keep taking turns. The first player to color all of the squares in his or her column wins the game.

Follow-the-Directions Math Story Mats © 2012 by Ada Goren, Scholastic Teaching Resources

Cat's Calendar

Mee-ay!

What is Cat's favorite month?

Sunday	Monday	Tuesday	Wednesday	Thursday	Friday	Saturday
		1	2	3	4	5
6	7	8	9	10	11	12
13	14	15	16	17	18	19
20	21	22	23	24	25	26
27	28	29	30	31		

Sunday	Monday	Tuesday	Wednesday
Thursday	Friday	Saturday	

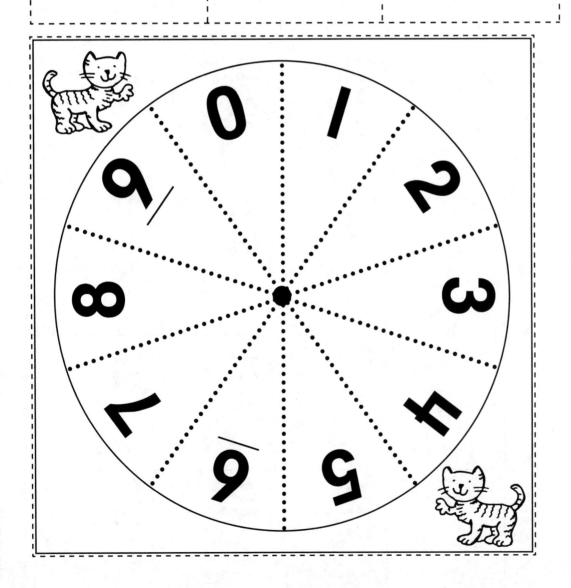

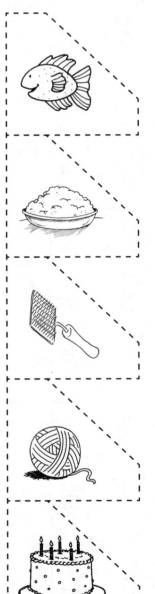

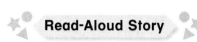

Penny's Sweets

Skill

Nonstandard Units
of Measurement

✦ Read-Aloud Story

Materials

read-aloud story (page 70)
story mat (page 71)
peppermint rulers (page 72)

Getting Ready

Copy, color, and cut out a story mat and a peppermint ruler for each child in
a small group. Laminate the pieces for durability.

Using the Story Mat

Give each child a story mat and a peppermint ruler. Ask children to listen as you
read aloud the story the first time. Then read the story again. Pause as you go
along, giving children time to use their story mats and rulers to solve the problems.

Talk About It

✱ Which candy measures the most in peppermint units? Which measures
the least?

✱ What is the difference—in peppermint units—between the length of the candy
bar and the length of the licorice stick? How can you find the answer?

✦ Story-Mat Game

Materials (for 2–4 players)

read-aloud story (page 70)
story mat (page 71)
measurement cards (page 72)
peppermint rulers (page 72)
plastic chips (six per player)

Getting Ready

Copy, cut out, and laminate the game directions and four sets of the measurement
cards. Use the story mats and peppermint rulers that were prepared for the story-
mat activity, or prepare additional rulers for the game.

Playing the Game

Give each player a story mat, peppermint ruler, and six plastic chips (to use as
game markers). Shuffle the measurement cards and stack them facedown in the
center of the table. Then read the directions and model how to play the game.
If desired, play it with children the first time.

Penny's Sweets

At Penny's Sweets, the candy is priced in an unusual way. Each piece of candy costs the same number of pennies as its measurement in peppermint units! Customers must measure each piece of candy to find its cost.

Molly came in to buy a licorice stick. Use your peppermint ruler to measure the candy. How many peppermint units long is it? How much will it cost?

Next, Dan came in with five pennies. Which candy can he buy? Use your ruler to find out. Tell its measurement in peppermint units. Then Amie came in to buy a piece of candy corn and a lollipop. Measure each candy and tell how many peppermint units tall it is. How many pennies does Amie need to buy both?

Malik wants to buy gummy bears. He has four pennies. How tall is the gummy bear? How many gummy bears can he buy? Now measure the peanut-butter cup. How many peppermint units long is it? Can Malik buy the peanut-butter cup instead of the gummy bears?

Penny's Sweets

Players: 2–4

How to Play

1. Take a card from the stack. What is the measurement on it? Find the candy on your mat that matches the measurement. Use your peppermint ruler.

2. When you find a match, place a marker on that candy. Then put your card at the bottom of the stack.

3. Keep taking turns. If a candy has already been measured and marked, you may not put another marker on it.

4. The first player to place a marker on all of his or her candy wins the game.

Follow-the-Directions Math Story Mats © 2012 by Ada Goren, Scholastic Teaching Resources

Penny's Sweets Story Mat

Peppermint Rulers and Measurement Cards

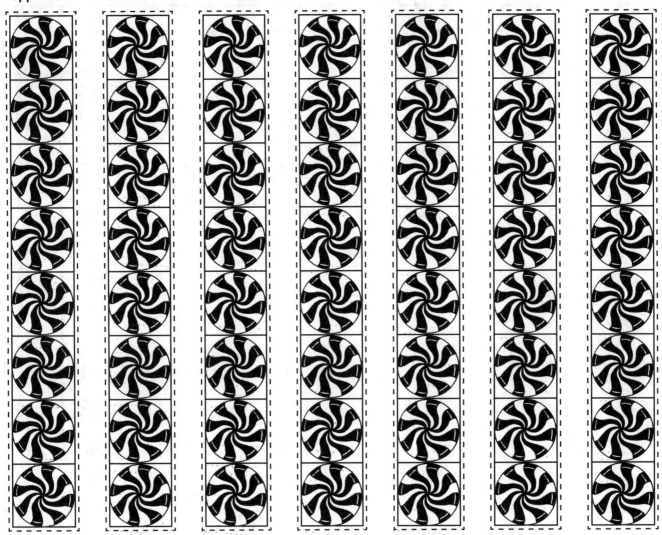

8 peppermint units	**2** peppermint units	**4** peppermint units
5 peppermint units	**6** peppermint units	**1** peppermint units

Full-Month Math Discoveries Made Easy © 2012 by Ada Goren, Scholastic Teaching Resources (page 72)

Snakes Rule!

 Read-Aloud Story

Materials

read-aloud story (page 74)
story mat (page 75)
snake rulers (page 76)

Getting Ready

Copy, color, and cut out a story mat and a snake ruler for
each child in a small group. Laminate the pieces for durability.

Using the Story Mat

Give each child a story mat and a snake ruler. Ask children to listen as you read
aloud the story the first time. Then read the story again. Pause as you go along,
giving children time to use their story mats and rulers to solve the problems.

Talk About It

* Which flower in the garden is the tallest? Which is the shortest? What is the
  difference—in inches—in their heights?

* What is the difference—in inches—between the height of the flagpost and
  the flower under the flag?

Story-Mat Game

Materials (for 2 players)

game directions (page 74)
story mat (page 75)
flower cards (page 76)
snake rulers (page 76)
paper bag

Getting Ready

Copy, cut out, and laminate the game directions and a set of flower cards. Use
the story mats and snake rulers that were prepared for the story-mat activity, or
prepare additional rulers for the game.

Playing the Game

Give each player a story mat and snake ruler. Put the flower cards in the paper
bag. Place the bag in the center of the table. Then read the directions and model
how to play the game. If desired, play it with children the first time. Players can
make tally marks on scraps of paper to keep their own score.

Snakes Rule!

Hissy Snake just loves to measure things, so it's a good thing that each stripe on his body measures one inch wide! He's in the flower garden today to measure the height of the flowers.

Hissy slithers to the flower nearest the flagpole. Help him measure that flower. How tall is it in inch units? Hissy moves on to the next flower. How many inches tall is that flower? Is it taller or shorter than the first flower?

Now Hissy measures the middle flower. What is its height? Give your answer in inch units. Hissy slides over to the fourth flower. How tall do you think that flower is? Guess, then help Hissy measure it. How many inches tall is the flower? Did you guess correctly?

Hissy reaches the last flower. Is it taller or shorter than the first flower? How tall do you think it is? Measure to find out. Finally, Hissy slithers back to the flagpole. Help him measure to find out how tall in inches the pole is.

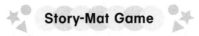
Story-Mat Game

Snakes Rule!

Players: 2

How to Play

1. Take a card out of the bag and look at the flower. Find the matching flower on your mat.

2. Measure the flower. Use your snake ruler. How many inches tall is the flower?

3. After each player takes a turn, compare your measurements. Is your flower the taller of the two? If so, you earn one point.

4. Put the flower cards back in the bag. Then keep taking turns and comparing your measurements. The first player to earn 5 points wins.

Follow-the-Directions Math Story Mats © 2012 by Ada Goren, Scholastic Teaching Resources

Snakes Rule! Story Mat

Snake Rulers and Flower Cards

| 1 | 2 | 3 | 4 | 5 | 6 | 7 |

| 7 | 6 | 5 | 4 | 3 | 2 | 1 |

| 1 | 2 | 3 | 4 | 5 | 6 | 7 |

Freeze's Flavors

 Read-Aloud Story

Materials

read-aloud story (page 78)
story mat (page 79)
ice cream cards (page 80)

Getting Ready

Copy, color, and cut out a story mat and two sets of
ice cream cards for each child in a small group.
Laminate the pieces for durability.

Using the Story Mat

Give each child a story mat and two sets of ice cream cards. Ask children to
listen as you read aloud the story the first time. Then read the story again.
Pause as you go along, giving children time to use their story mats and cards
to solve the problems.

Talk About It

✳ Was it easy or difficult to tell which flavor was the favorite?

✳ What is another way to show the results from the chart?

✳ How can you find out what ice cream flavor is the class favorite?

Assessment TIPS

- Observe if children
  place their scoops in
  the correct columns
  on the chart.

- Check that children are
  able to interpret and
  understand the results
  of their chart.

- For the game, check
  that children count
  the correct number of
  scoops on each spin.

Story-Mat Game

Materials (for 2–4 players)

game directions (page 78)   brass fastener
story mat (page 79)   paper clip
ice cream cards (page 80)   coin
game spinner (page 80)

Getting Ready

Copy, cut out, and laminate the game directions and game spinner. Attach the
paper clip to the spinner with the brass fastener, as shown on page 5. Use the
story mats and ice cream cards that were prepared for the story-mat activity, or
prepare additional cards for the game.

Playing the Game

Give each player a story mat and two sets of ice cream cards. Place the spinner
and coin in the center of the table. Then read the directions and model how to
play the game. If desired, play it with children the first time.

Freeze's Flavors

Fred and Freda Freeze own an ice cream shop named Freeze's Flavors. One Monday, they posted a chart for customers to fill in with their favorite flavors. By the end of the day, there were 3 scoops in the vanilla column, 8 scoops in the chocolate column, and 6 scoops in the strawberry column. Fill in the chart with the scoops. Each scoop stands for one customer's favorite. Which flavor was the favorite for that day? Clear the scoops off of the mat.

The Freeze's posted the chart again on Thursday. By closing time that day, there were 5 scoops for vanilla, 4 for chocolate, and 4 for strawberry. Which was the favorite flavor on Thursday? How many more people liked vanilla ice cream better than chocolate? Clear the scoops off of the mat.

The chart was posted again on Saturday. That day, 2 people voted for vanilla, 7 for chocolate, and 5 for strawberry. Put a scoop in the column for your favorite flavor. Which flavor was the favorite for that day?

Freeze's Flavors

Players: 2–4

How to Play

1. Spin the spinner. What flavor did it land on? Find that flavor on your mat.

2. Toss the coin. Did it land on heads or on tails?

   • If heads, put two scoops in the column for your flavor.

   • If tails, put one scoop in the column.

3. Keep playing until each player has had four turns.

4. One player gives the spinner a final spin. What flavor did it land on? The player with the most scoops for that flavor wins the game.

Follow-the-Directions Math Story Mats © 2012 by Ada Goren, Scholastic Teaching Resources

Freeze's Flavors
Ice Cream Shop

Which flavor do you like the most?

Vanilla	Chocolate	Strawberry

Follow-the-Directions Math Story Mats © 2012 by Ada Goren, Scholastic Teaching Resources (page 79)

Ice Cream Cards and Game Spinner

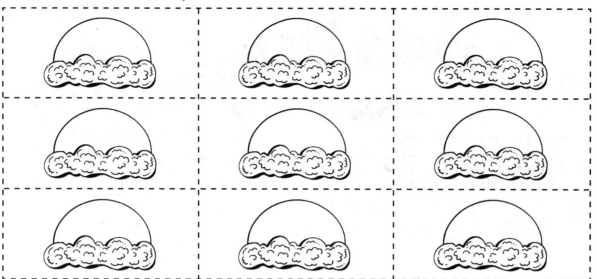

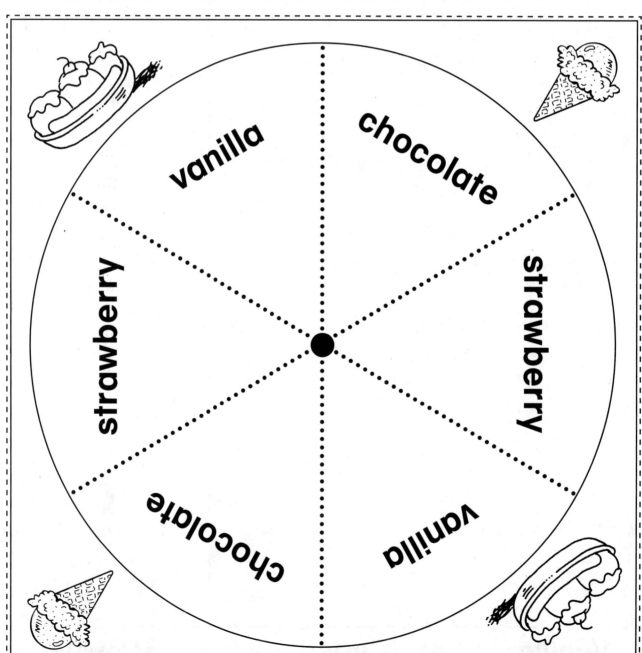